BEACON

mesozoic mass extinction iridium

Dinosaurs

Chicxulub catastrophism pterosaur tsunami

Éric Buffetaut

CASSELL&CO

***Triceratops:* a 300 gram (11 ounce) brain in a body of 6–9 tons.**

74

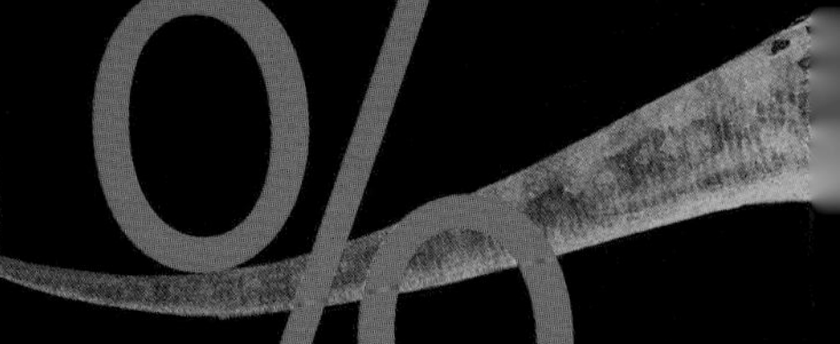

99% of the millions of species

that have existed since the appearance of the first living creatures are now extinct.

102

Dozens of theories have been put forward to explain the disappearance of the dinosaurs, including the downright weird: 'Noah's ark was too small for them', or 'An epidemic of cataracts made them go blind ...'

115

*It is estimated that on average the Earth is hit **every 100 million years by a meteorite measuring about 10 kilometres (6 miles) in diameter** and capable of producing a huge catastrophe like the one that happened at the boundary between the Cretaceous and Tertiary periods.*

113

1842

Richard Owen suggested the word ***dinosauria.*** 107

the smallest was 60 centimetres (2 feet)
the largest 30 metres (100 feet)
the lightweights weighed 25 kilograms (55 pounds) 72

74 **the heavyweights 60 tons.**

800

species of dinosaurs have been identified so far, divided into two large groups: the Saurischia and the Ornithischia. 67

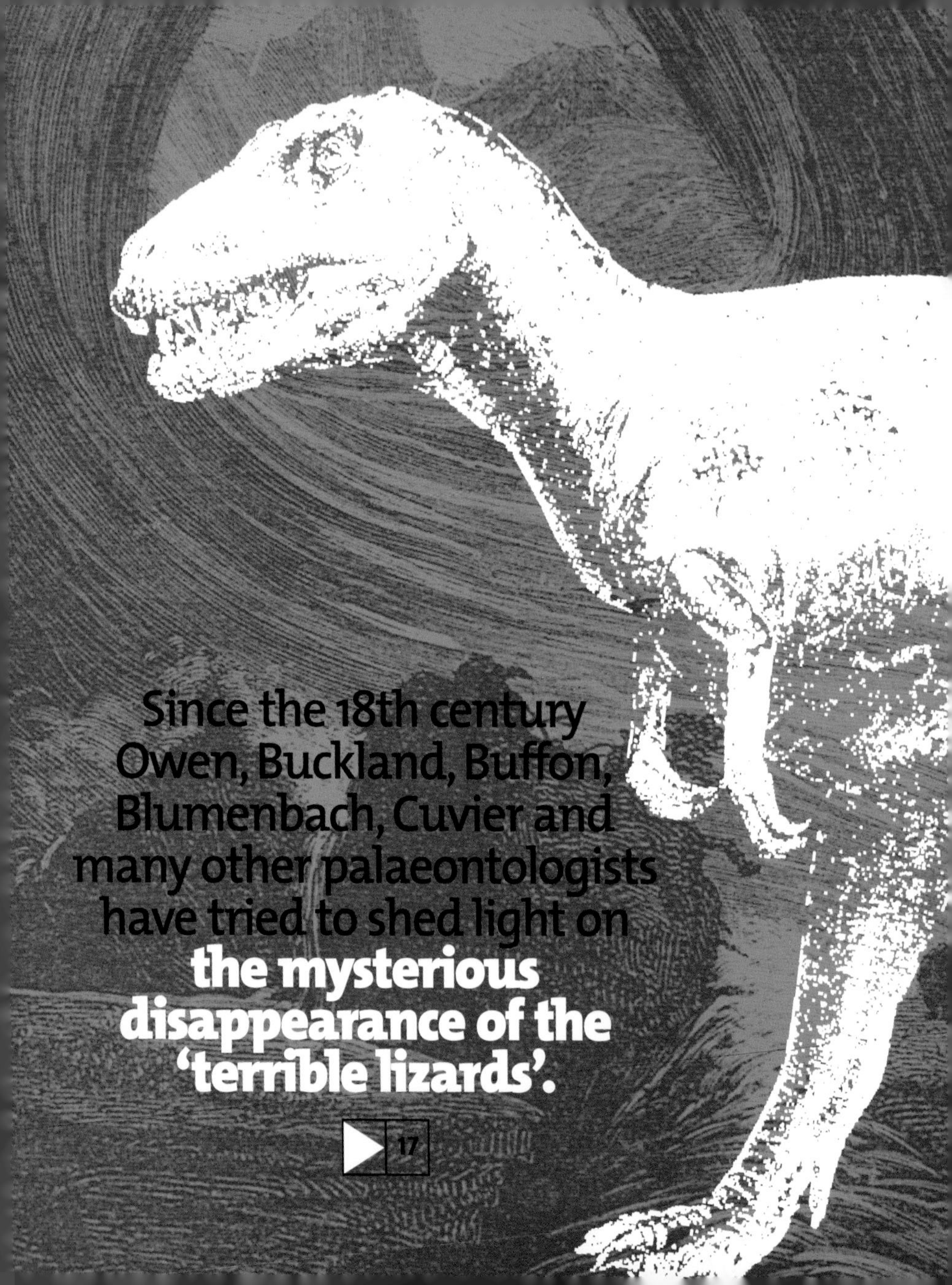

Since the 18th century Owen, Buckland, Buffon, Blumenbach, Cuvier and many other palaeontologists have tried to shed light on **the mysterious disappearance of the 'terrible lizards'.**

▶ 17

Who were the last dinosaurs?

▶ 72

Were dinosaurs cold-blooded?

There is some evidence that suggests some were not, as they could survive the temperatures of northern Alaska and the Antarctic, although these regions weren't as cold as they are today.

▶ 30

Nowadays palaeontologists think their disappearance was due to an **unfortunate accident.**

▶ 32

From meteorite material to the surface of the globe.

In 1980 the journal Science *published a crucial article on the origin of the layer of iridium discovered in the geological strata dating from a period some time between the Cretaceous and Tertiary eras. Since then, an increasing number of discoveries have pointed to dinosaurs having been the victims of a worldwide ecological catastrophe, caused by the impact of an enormous asteroid.*

▶ 35

All they left behind were tracks, teeth and fossilised skeletons.

▶ 30

104

'Perhaps we may yet come across some of those lizard-like creatures which scientists have been able to reconstruct from a fragment of bone or cartilage?'

Jules Verne,
Journey to the Centre of the Earth.

'And we were the kings of all the world
We knew its breadth and length;
We dwelt in the glory of solitude,
And the majesty of strength.'

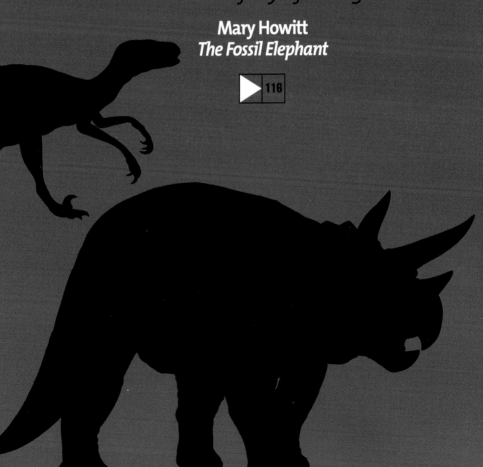

Mary Howitt
The Fossil Elephant

116

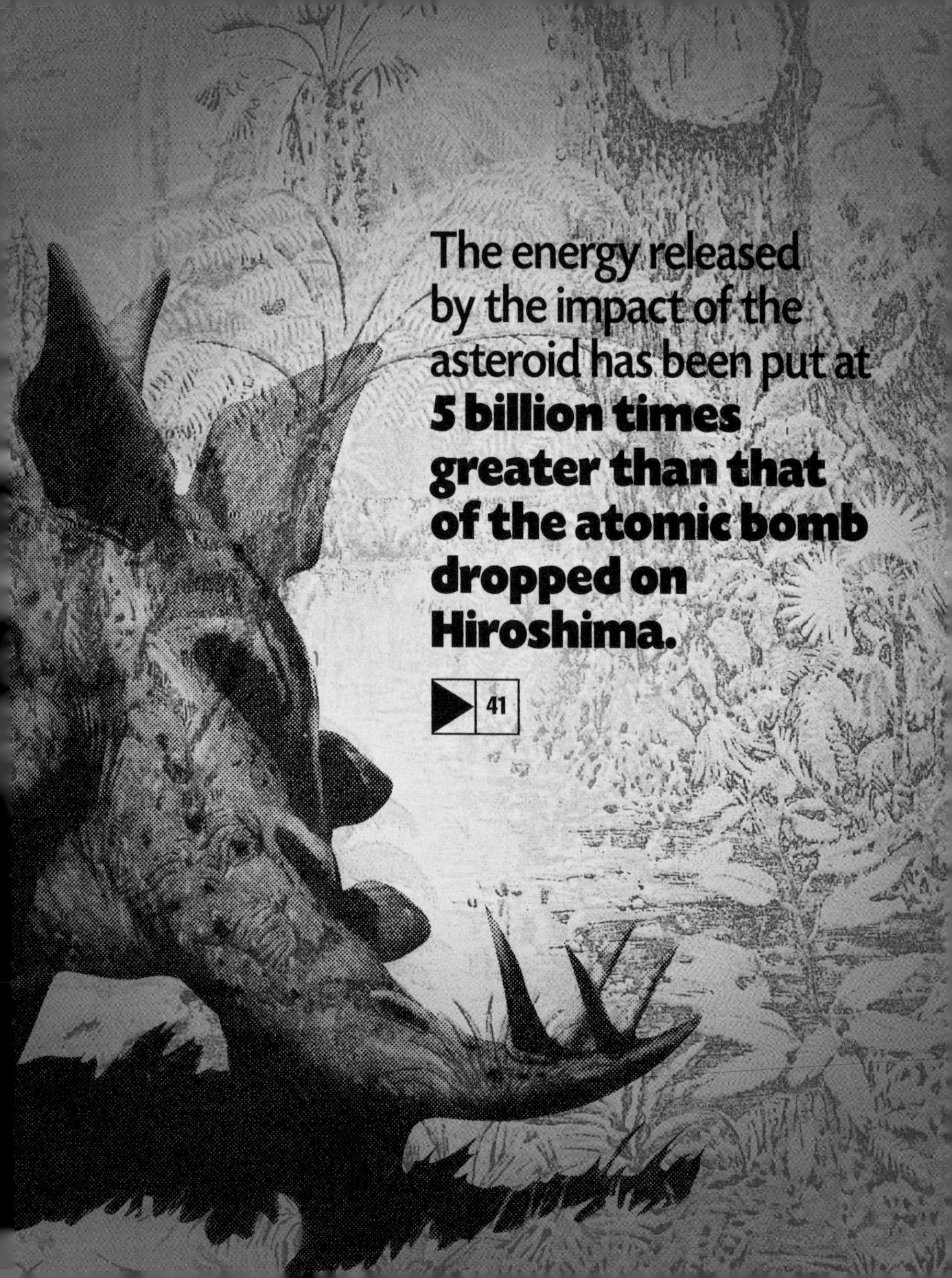

The energy released by the impact of the asteroid has been put at **5 billion times greater than that of the atomic bomb dropped on Hiroshima.**

▶ 41

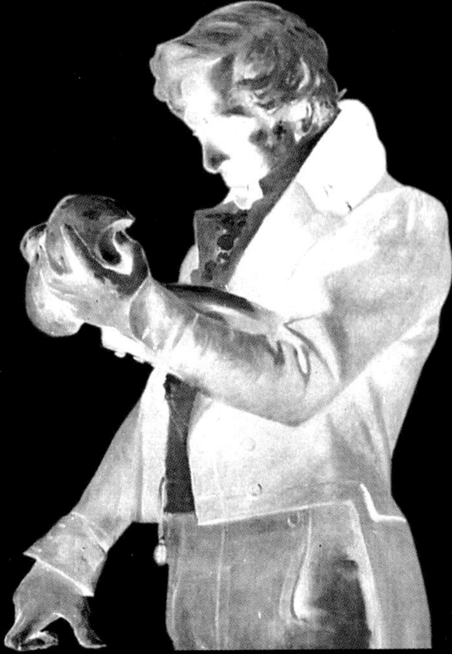

DISCOVER

FROM THE DISCOVERY OF FOSSILS BY 18TH-CENTURY NATURALISTS TO THE PALAEONTOLOGICAL INVESTIGATIONS OF THE PRESENT DAY, THERE HAS BEEN NO SHORTAGE OF EXPLANATIONS FOR THE DISAPPEARANCE OF THE DINOSAURS. WAS IT DRAWN OUT BUT IRREVERSIBLE, OR WAS IT SUDDEN AND VIOLENT? THE DISCOVERY IN THE 1980s OF A HUGE CRATER IN MEXICO PROVIDED NEW EVIDENCE TO SUPPORT THE ARGUMENT THAT IT WAS DUE TO THE IMPACT OF A GIANT ASTEROID.

What could be more extinct than a dinosaur? These animals are symbolic of the extinction of species to such an extent, that it is sometimes forgotten that their demise, 65 million years ago, brought to an end a very long history of successful evolution on their part. At times dinosaurs have been seen as an evolutionary failure, as if they had been maladjusted monsters, doomed to disappear. However, palaeontologists no longer see them in that light, and it is now thought that their disappearance was probably due more to an unfortunate accident than to any biological imperative.

The story of the dinosaurs began some 230 million years ago, during the first geological period of the Mesozoic era, called the Triassic. The dinosaurs that appeared then were generally small and not unlike other reptiles of the same period.

FRIGHTENING MONSTERS

The human imagination, especially in film or literature, has treated dinosaurs with an ambivalent mixture of fear and fascination.

AN EVOLUTIONARY SUCCESS STORY

Success was not long in coming to the dinosaurs. By the end of the Triassic period, 205 million years ago, they had become the dominant animals on all continents, displacing various other groups of reptiles. The earliest dinosaurs were lightly-built carnivores, two to three metres long (seven to ten feet), that used their sharp teeth to catch a variety of prey which probably included smaller, lizard-like reptiles, insects and other small animals. The hind legs were adapted for running, with the long limbs situated below the body to facilitate a smooth swinging gait, and an ankle that operated like a hinge. This type of ankle, and the habit of standing on the toes rather than on flat feet, were characteristic features of dinosaurs. The front limbs would not have been used while running, they were designed more for grasping, and sometimes had sharp claws, which were used to grab prey and hold on to it while eating.

In the late Triassic period the first plant-eating dinosaurs appeared. These forerunners of giants like the Diplodocus, spread rapidly across most of the world, perhaps because they were one of the few animals at that time to live on plants. The first plant-eaters were still mostly bipedal (ie they usually stood on their two hind legs), and had teeth that were designed for shredding plant material, rather than grinding tough food. Some were already giants almost ten metres (33 feet) long, whilst others gradually evolved into larger animals that needed to stand on all fours, and had elephant-like legs. The success of plant-eaters resulted in the evolution of a whole range of larger meat-eaters that preyed on them.

The next geological period, the Jurassic, which ended 130 million years ago, saw a continual diversification of the dinosaurs, which was due, at least in part, to the continual interaction between predators and their prey. To protect themselves from ever more powerful carnivores armed with formidable teeth and claws, some herbivores sought safety in flight, staying lean and fast-moving, while others developed a protective armour of scales and bony spines. Finally, as they developed and grew bigger, they reached sizes that were impressive enough to discourage most predators. By the end of the Jurassic period some plant-eating dinosaurs measured more than 30 metres (nearly 100 feet) in length, while others weighed in at almost 70 tons! From the Jurassic period onwards a group of small dinosaurs, their bodies covered in feathers, started on a conquest of the air – birds had arrived, and in the end would survive their non-flying relatives.

THE BREAK-UP OF THE ORIGINAL CONTINENT

In the Cretaceous period, which followed the Jurassic, the success of the dinosaurs showed no signs of abating even though the world around them was changing. From the beginning of the Jurassic period the continents, which in the Triassic period had been joined together in a single mass, started to break away from each other, driven apart by the movement of the tectonic plates. On these land masses, which continued to grow ever more isolated from each other, new and different types of dinosaurs began to appear. The rest of the natural world was also changing. During the Cretaceous period one of the greatest revolutions in the history of the plant kingdom took place: flowering plants appeared, profoundly changing the landscape, which until then had been dominated by ferns and conifers. Through all these upheavals, dinosaurs successfully continued to evolve and adapt.

A FOREST OF THE DISTANT PAST

Changes in the plant world over millions of years have had a profound influence on the evolution of the animal world.

The mystery surrounding the dinosaurs is that 65 million years ago they were flourishing when, suddenly they vanished, a puzzle that has long taxed the brains of the greatest palaeontologists. The mystery was further compounded because numerous other groups of animals that had also lived in the lands and seas of the Mesozoic period disappeared along with them.

THE SEARCH FOR LOST SPECIES

Everybody knows that countless species of living creatures, from dodos to dinosaurs and mammoths, have become extinct over the passage of time. However, this has not always been universally believed. Up until the end of the 18th century, for example, the possibility that a living species could totally disappear posed a rather tricky problem for scholars and philosophers. The very idea that animals or plants could vanish from the face of the earth contradicted the concept that Nature, as created by God, was good and perfect (even if Man,

endowed with free will, was sinful). How was it possible that the Creator could have allowed some elements of his creation to disappear?

And yet naturalists, studying fossils – animal and plant remains preserved in rock – were making strange discoveries. Some of these sea or land creatures, which must have lived in the distant past (even if nobody could yet date them precisely) bore no resemblance to any living creatures then known. Scientists speculated that they were species which no longer lived in the European regions where their fossils had been discovered, but which would one day be found living in the darkest forests of the Americas or Africa, or even in the depths of the oceans. Some people continued to believe this right up to the beginning of the 19th century, but expeditions to the different corners of the globe finally forced them to abandon this hope, even though plenty of undreamt-of animals, from the giant panda to the okapi, were being brought back to Europe. Others thought that man may have been responsible for the extermination of some of these lost species, as people became aware of the destructive capacity of human beings. Nevertheless, knowledge of animal anatomy moved on, and the more that was learned about present-day species, the clearer it became that certain fossils did not resemble them at all. More daring thinkers did not shirk from drawing the obvious conclusion. The English scholar, Robert Hooke (1635–1703), had already admitted that many species known in their fossilised state could no longer be found in nature today. A few decades later Georges-Louis Leclerc, the Count of Buffon (1707–1788), setting out to reconstruct the 'epochs of nature', had to admit that in the course of time certain species had become extinct, victims of the planet's cooling, he supposed. A generation later, the 19th century German naturalist, Johann Friedrich Blumenbach (1752–1840), suggested that major upheavals on the surface of the globe had been responsible for wiping out whole groups of animals.

CUVIER AND COMPARATIVE ANATOMY

THE ADVENT OF PALAEONTOLOGY

The work of Georges Cuvier laid the foundations for comparative anatomy and scientific palaeontology.

However, the true scale of the extinction of the species phenomenon was shown irrefutably, and convincingly enough to silence the remaining sceptics, by Georges Cuvier (1769–1832). His success came through the use of comparative anatomy, a research method he was chiefly responsible for developing. Cuvier was not only able to give precise details of the make-up of the fossilised species, but also to show how these differed from contemporary species. By using this technique Cuvier was able to show, in 1796, that the mammoth and the mastodon were different from present-day elephants and that the species to which they belonged were no longer found anywhere in the world. Scientific palaeontology and the study of extinct species developed side-by-side. To the amazement of his contemporaries, Cuvier discovered a large number of previously unknown creatures. Like Blumenbach, he believed that the main causes of the disappearance of these creatures had to be far-reaching disasters which, on more than one occasion, had devastated the Earth.

Among the many extinct animals to be discovered, were the large, strange reptiles whose remains, first unearthed in England, started to attract the attention of scholars in the 1820s. William Buckland described the Megalosaurus in 1824 and Gideon Mantell wrote about the Iguanodon in 1825. As yet there was no mention of the term 'dinosaurs'; the word (from the Greek *deinos*, terrible, and *sauros*, lizard) was not used until 1842 by another British palaeontologist, Richard Owen. Cuvier, however, who followed these discoveries with interest, could already see, in the extinction of these great land-based reptiles (as well as of their marine and airborne contemporaries), one of the greatest interruptions in the history of living creatures, what he called the 'global revolutions'. Later research would confirm his view, and it was the English geologist, John Phillips, who identified this unexpected break as occurring at the boundary between two great geological eras, the Mesozoic (era of 'middle' life) and the Cenozoic (era of 'recent' life).

THE THEORY OF CATASTROPHISM

As far as Cuvier and some of his successors were concerned, the reason for this great extinction at the end of the Mesozoic era was a generalised disaster, one of the terrifying events that have punctuated the history of the world. This catastrophist vision of the Earth's past reached its peak during the first decades of the 19th century. Some people saw in it a means of reconciling geology with a more or less literal reading of the Bible; could Noah's Flood not be interpreted as the most recent of the catastrophes? If it was divine intervention, then no further explanation was necessary. The French geologist, Alcide d'Orbigny (1802–1857), went so far as to propose a history of precisely 27 catastrophes, wiping out all life on the planet on each occasion, to be followed by a new creation each time. Some geologists, however, queried these unprovable assumptions. Already, in the 18th century, the Scottish geologist James Hutton had suggested that the transformations of our globe took place gradually as a result of the same forces that we can still see acting today: the slow erosion of the land, deposition of sedimentary rocks, gradual variations in sea levels and so on. Geological phenomena brought about by small changes accumulating over immensely long periods of time can produce huge effects. Towards the middle of the 19th century the idea began to be generally accepted. Global catastrophes were

VISION OF A CATASTROPHE

An illustration of the Great Flood as traditionally imagined.

no longer needed in this 'uniformitarian' vision of natural forces at work, the most famous champion of which was the Scottish geologist Charles Lyell (1795–1875).

Charles Darwin (1809–1892) was following a similar train of thought when he put forward his theory of evolution by natural selection in 1859. In his opinion, too, developments in the living world had come about gradually. In each generation of animals or plants there was some variation between individuals. Those individuals best adapted to the conditions tended to survive and breed. The next generation was like these parents, but with its own variations. Over generations new species could arise by a gradual shift away from the ancestral type. Although Darwin's followers acknowledged the presence of violence in the struggle for existence, Cuvier's catastrophes had little place in it. However, the question of the extinctions remained, even if the palaeontologists, most of whom had rapidly become evolutionists by now, were more interested in the actual appearance and subsequent development of species than in their end. After all, what was surprising about the fact that in the universal struggle for existence, innumerable species should have perished in competition with animals or plants that had adapted themselves more successfully.

ANATOMIST AND PALAEONTOLOGIST

After the discovery of large reptile fossils in England, Richard Owen suggested calling these animals 'dinosaurs'.

THE PLOT THICKENS

When Richard Owen introduced the word dinosaur in 1842 he did so chiefly on the basis of three different large reptile fossils, all found in England. However, the progress of palaeontological research worldwide soon added greatly to the number of finds. In the final decades of the 19th century, spectacular discoveries, particularly in the American West, gradually revealed the great diversity of this group of animals, and confirmed its pre-eminent place in the fauna of the Mesozoic era. The discoveries continue today; indeed, they have multiplied over the last twenty years or so, ensuring that dinosaurs remain as popular with palaeontologists as with the public at large. Our image of dinosaurs has changed a great deal since 1842. We now know that they were far more complex creatures than simply over-developed lizards, and we have a much better understanding of their anatomy and evolution, and even of their behaviour. However, one significant fact predicted by Cuvier's theories has been confirmed. Their disappearance took place at one of the great cut-off points in the history of the natural world – the end of the Cretaceous period. After reigning supreme for more than 150 million years, the dinosaurs simply disappeared. No further traces of them could be found in the geological strata of the Tertiary period, which followed the Cretaceous. Explanations, however, haven't been slow in coming. Indeed, the sheer number of theories alone is proof of

5
3
1
2
9
12
13
6
14
7
VERMORCKEN.

the interest raised by the problem, as well as the difficulties encountered in resolving it. Not all are worth taking equally seriously but, even when you ignore the most far-fetched explanations, a good number remain that have continued to attract the attention of serious scientists and are, on occasion, the subject of lively debate. One of the difficulties palaeontologists face is that it is extremely difficult to find a classic Darwinian explanation for this disappearance, for if dinosaurs were vanquished in the struggle for existence, then who were the conquerors?

COMPETITION FROM MAMMALS

Following the demise of the dinosaurs, the development of mammals during the Cenozoic period was staggering. They diversified in all directions and conquered one environment after another, from the air to the oceans. But is it really conceivable that these masters of the modern world could have caused the dinosaurs to become extinct 65 million years ago? This is hard to believe, for the simple reason that the largest mammals alive at the time of the dinosaurs were no bigger than a badger, and were hardly likely to represent much of a threat. Some palaeontologists have assumed that mammals, too small to attack the dinosaurs themselves, must have raided their nests for eggs. This theory suggests that, by devouring their offspring before they were hatched, the mammals were able to bring about the downfall of creatures many times their size. There is, nevertheless, one major problem with this theory: mammals and dinosaurs appeared more or less at the same time in the Upper Triassic period, and thus lived side-by-side for at least 160 million years, without either causing the disappearance of the other. It is also difficult to see why mammals should suddenly have developed an insatiable appetite for dinosaur eggs after so long. And there is another reason why this theory is unconvincing: this was disaster on a huge scale. What about the numerous other living organisms that disappeared at the same time as the dinosaurs? There can have been no possible link between the activities of mammals and the extinction of ammonites and belemnites, molluscs that lived in the sea and became extinct at the same time. The weak point of many of the theories that claim to explain the end of the dinosaurs is precisely this: they overlook the other victims of what is now often referred to as 'the mass extinction of the Cretaceous-Tertiary boundary'.

THE AGE OF THE REPTILES

The discoveries of the early 19th century soon revealed to palaeontologists that the Mesozoic had been an era dominated by reptiles.

MASS EXTINCTION

Other large reptiles disappeared at the same time as the dinosaurs. Some of them, the pterosaurs, were flying creatures. Appearing first in the Triassic period, they enjoyed a long

evolutionary history throughout the Jurassic and Cretaceous periods. At the end of the Cretaceous period some pterosaurs had evolved into immense flying creatures, with a wingspan reaching up to about ten metres (33 feet) – the size of a small aeroplane. A membrane stretching from a very elongated fourth finger to their hind legs made it possible for them to fly. Their remains have been found up to the final levels of the Cretaceous period, after which they disappeared. In the sea, two groups of large reptiles also became extinct at the boundary between the Cretaceous period and the Tertiary. One group, the plesiosaurs, had an equally long history, as their first appearance was also in the Triassic. Typically, these were animals whose limbs had been transformed into flippers; their bodies were short and wide, and they had short tails and very long necks, ending in small heads with jaws full of pointed teeth to enable them to capture fish or molluscs. The mosasaurs, on the other hand, were relatively new arrivals, appearing at the beginning of the Upper Cretaceous period, about 90 million years ago. They were in fact gigantic lizards adapted to life in the sea, with flippers as limbs and a snake-like body. Their long jaws, armed with strong teeth, meant they were capable of attacking large prey.

A FLYING REPTILE

This old, rather fanciful illustration is not very accurate. It shows a pterodactyl – a flying reptile that was a contemporary of the dinosaurs and whose existence was discovered by Cuvier.

While these huge reptiles, with their spectacular appearance, have come to symbolise the mass extinction that took place at the end of the Cretaceous period, they were far from being the only victims. For palaeontologists more interested in invertebrates than vertebrates, the significant event of this period was the disappearance of the ammonites and belemnites. These were cephalopod molluscs, related to today's octopus, cuttlefish and nautilus, and their fossils are commonly found in Mesozoic rocks. The ammonites possessed a spiral shell similar to that of the nautilus, while the belemnites, which externally resembled squid, had an internal shell that looked very much like a bullet. These two groups, which flourished in the Mesozoic era, also became extinct at the time of the Cretaceous-Tertiary boundary.

OTHER KINDS OF LIFE

However, the picture conjured up of this great extinction would not be complete if it were restricted to the animals that disappeared. Other kinds of life were also decimated, so that at the beginning of the Tertiary period only a few individual species survived. The most striking examples of these are the planktonic foraminifera. These tiny, single-celled organisms covered with shells of calcium formed an important part of the marine plankton and floated in vast numbers near the surface of the sea at the end of the Cretaceous period. They were almost completely wiped out at the same time as the dinosaurs. As thousands of specimens of these microscopic creatures can be found in a small piece of rock, specialists in micro-palaeontology have been able to carry out very precise studies of the mass (but not total) extinction of the planktonic foraminifera.

It is estimated that almost 70 per cent of the species that were living at the end of the Cretaceous period were annihilated by this phase of extinction. The creatures affected lived in very different environments, so the obvious question is what a dinosaur weighing several tons and a microscopic foraminifer could possibly have in common. To produce a realistic and convincing theory to explain the great extinction that took place, we need to understand why some organisms – ranging from insects to mammals and including tortoises and crocodiles – survived. Because, of course, there were survivors, including our own distant ancestors.

A GRADUAL DETERIORATION OF THE ENVIRONMENT?

In line with the uniformitarian principles that have governed Earth sciences since the mid-19th century, many palaeontologists have attempted to explain this particular extinction by causes that were slow and gradual, believing these to be the most probable. In one form or another these theories assume a gradual environmental decline, in particular, of the climate during the last millions of years of the Cretaceous period, that proved fatal to dinosaurs and other creatures. Why should the climate have deteriorated in this way? It is common knowledge that ice ages occurred on several occasions in the history of our planet – cold periods during which the polar ice caps and mountain glaciers spread out to cover immense areas. Our ancestor, prehistoric man, was witness to the last glaciation, since the last major ice age took place only some 12,000 years ago. Did an ice age, therefore, cause the end of the dinosaurs? The answer is quite definitely no; the traces that glaciers leave behind in rocks are familiar to geologists, and nothing of this sort has been discovered in Cretaceous-Tertiary boundary deposits. In fact the Cretaceous period and the beginning of the Tertiary were generally warm periods during which there were no ice caps at the poles; dinosaurs even lived as far north as the most northerly reaches of Alaska and in the Antarctic during the Upper Cretaceous period.

LETHAL CLOUDS

The theory of cataclysmic volcanic activity suggests the emission of massive clouds of terrible asphyxiating gases.

Since there is no question of it having been a glacial period, could more subtle changes in the environment have resulted in disastrous effects on certain species? One theory which has many supporters, in particular the palaeontologist Leonard Ginsburg, Paris, holds that the mass extinction was caused by a generalised lowering of sea levels. Such marine regressions frequently occurred during the history of our planet. They had a variety of causes: in the case

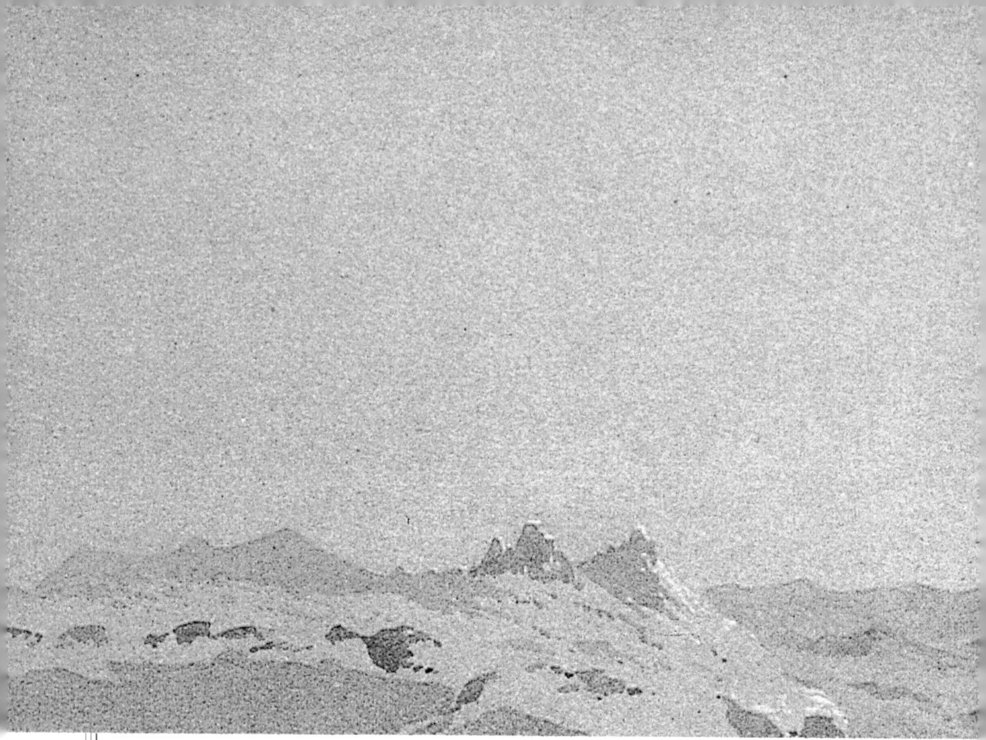

of a glacial period, so much water was captured by the polar caps in the form of ice that the level of the world's seas sometimes dropped by 20–30 metres (roughly 70–100 feet) or more. In between the ice ages, the occurence of regressions and transgressions (which are the rises in sea level), can be explained by the variations in volume of the oceans' basins caused by plate tectonics. Geologists have long confirmed that a regression occurred shortly before the end of the Cretaceous period.

The scenario is as follows: a substantial drop in sea level, perhaps of more than 100 metres (330 feet), dries out a large part of the continental shelf around the emerging ground. This creates very hostile conditions in countless shallow marine habitats for the creatures that live there. As a result, a large number of marine species disappear. On the new land the climate changes, becoming more continental as the total surface of the exposed continents has now increased. A more continental climate means there is a greater contrast between the seasons, with colder winters and warmer summers, which the dinosaurs cannot adapt to, and therefore perish.

WHAT ROLE DID THE CLIMATE PLAY?

On a number of occasions radical shifts in the global climate have caused ice ages. But at the end of the Cretaceous period the climate was distinctly warmer than it is today.

MARINE REGRESSION

This explanation may seem plausible, and it certainly found favour with a number of palaeontologists. However, all scientific theories must be submitted to tests. For example, does the theory of regression correctly explain the palaeontological facts? There is no doubt that geological findings do confirm the existence of a regression towards the end of the Cretaceous period. It is probable, then, that the variations in sea level had an influence on the evolution of living creatures through the geographical and environmental changes they brought about, but could they have caused a mass extinction on the scale we are talking about? There is nothing to indicate this, and we should bear in mind that in the course of the dinosaurs' long history, several large-scale regressions took place without causing mass extinctions of these animals – the ones at the end of the Triassic and Jurassic periods, for example. Why, then, should the drop in sea level at the end of the Cretaceous period have had such different and disastrous effects? There is, however, a more serious question: the regression theory suggests a number of consequences that have not been borne out by palaeontological evidence – quite the opposite, in fact. It predicts, in particular, that the organisms most badly affected in the seas would be those living at the bottom, on the continental shelf. And yet exactly the opposite happened: the worst extinctions took place among the planktonic organisms which floated near the surface and which should not have been particularly affected by any loss of habitats on the sea bed, while the benthic animals, ie those living on the sea bed, were the least affected. The regression theory, therefore, does not clear this first crucial hurdle.

DINOSAURS IN A COLD CLIMATE

The regression theory assumed that dinosaurs were especially sensitive to climatic changes and incapable of surviving in a climate that had become more continental. This also contradicts palaeontological data, for two reasons. First of all, we know that some reptiles found today (tortoises, lizards, snakes and crocodiles), with whose physiology and ecology we are familiar, survived the crisis of the Cretaceous-Tertiary boundary. We know that these cold-blooded animals, ie whose internal temperature varies according to their surroundings, are not very good at surviving in extreme temperatures. Crocodiles, in particular, are now confined to tropical and subtropical regions, because they cannot endure harsh winters. They had no difficulty, however, in surviving the crisis of the Cretaceous-Tertiary boundary, the implication of which must be that the climate fluctuations cannot have been that dramatic. And yet the advocates of the marine regression theory hold that dinosaurs all over the world were the victims of a severe deterioration in climatic conditions. How, then, would crocodiles have survived this deterioration, if it wiped out dinosaurs from the Equator to the poles? The fact that polar dinosaurs existed has already been mentioned. In northern Alaska, for example, dinosaur remains have been discovered in the sediments of the Upper Cretaceous period, deposited in a climate which, while not glacial, must have been quite cool, since neither tortoises nor crocodiles lived this far north. We still don't know as much about the physiology of dinosaurs as we would like, but it seems clear that they were not restricted to tropical climates. If that is the case, how could a worsening climate that failed to kill off the crocodile population, result in the worldwide loss of dinosaurs? Here again, the theory of a regression having caused a fatal alteration to the climate, does not hold up.

Whatever gradual cause, spread over millions of years, is invoked to explain the disappearance

MASTERS OF THE SKY AND SEA

Pterosaurs and plesiosaurs – reptiles of the air and sea respectively – were victims of the same mass extinction that killed the dinosaurs.

of dinosaurs and numerous other species, it never quite succeeds in explaining everything. It has sometimes been claimed that there had been a decline in the number of different dinosaurs over the last few millions of years of the Cretaceous period, and that by the end of it no more than a handful of species remained. However, every year new species of dinosaur from the end of the Cretaceous period are discovered by palaeontologists. Eminent researchers in the field, such as Jean Le Loeuff, of the Espéraza Dinosaur Museum, France, estimate that several hundreds of species of dinosaurs existed worldwide at that time. This also applies to other groups of organisms that disappeared simultaneously, whether ammonites or plankton:

there is no indication at all that there was any significant decline during the several million years preceding the end of the Mesozoic era.

By the end of the 1970s research had reached an impasse. It was then that an unexpected discovery opened up new horizons and gave rise, from 1980 onwards, to a new theory and to much heated debate. This was no less than a return to good old-fashioned Catastrophism.

CATASTROPHE FROM OUTER SPACE

If the traditional gradualist explanations were unconvincing, why not then consider an event that was much more sudden and violent – a real example of catastrophism? Until recently few scientists had dared to volunteer new catastrophism theories since this line of thinking had had a bad press since the beginning of the 19th century. It was too easily associated with the pseudo-scientific ranting that ran up against the most well-proven facts of astronomy or geology. In 1956, however, a palaeontologist from Oregon, MW De Laubenfels, who specialised in fossilised sponges, was bold enough to publish a short article in a well-respected palaeontology journal in which he expounded a further theory on the disappearance of the dinosaurs. In his opinion the most probable explanation was that they were victims of the cataclysmic effects of the impact of a huge meteorite. With hindsight, the article was daring, as well as prophetic – but it was purely theoretical and didn't offer any tangible proof of the impact, and so passed unnoticed at the time.

AMMONITE FOSSIL

Ammonites – marine molluscs with a spiral shell – disappeared at the same time as the dinosaurs.

EXTRATERRESTRIAL MATERIAL

Towards the end of the 1970s, however, there were new developments. The American geologist, Walter Alvarez, of the University of California at Berkeley, was studying rocks in the Apennines, near Gubbio, in Italy, which had originally been formed in deep water. These sedimentary rocks dated from the end of the Cretaceous period and the beginning of the Tertiary, and one of the questions that intrigued him was how much time it took these sedimentary strata to form deposits.

The measurement of time has always been one of the great problems of geology. To estimate the length of time a deposit takes to form, you need some sort of natural chronometer, something that is both constant and measurable. At the suggestion of his father, Luis Alvarez, a physics Nobel prize winner, Walter became interested in meteorite material in rocks. It is a known fact that the Earth is bombarded by a stream of material from space, mostly in the form of minute pieces the size of grains of sand, larger meteorites being much rarer. If you assume

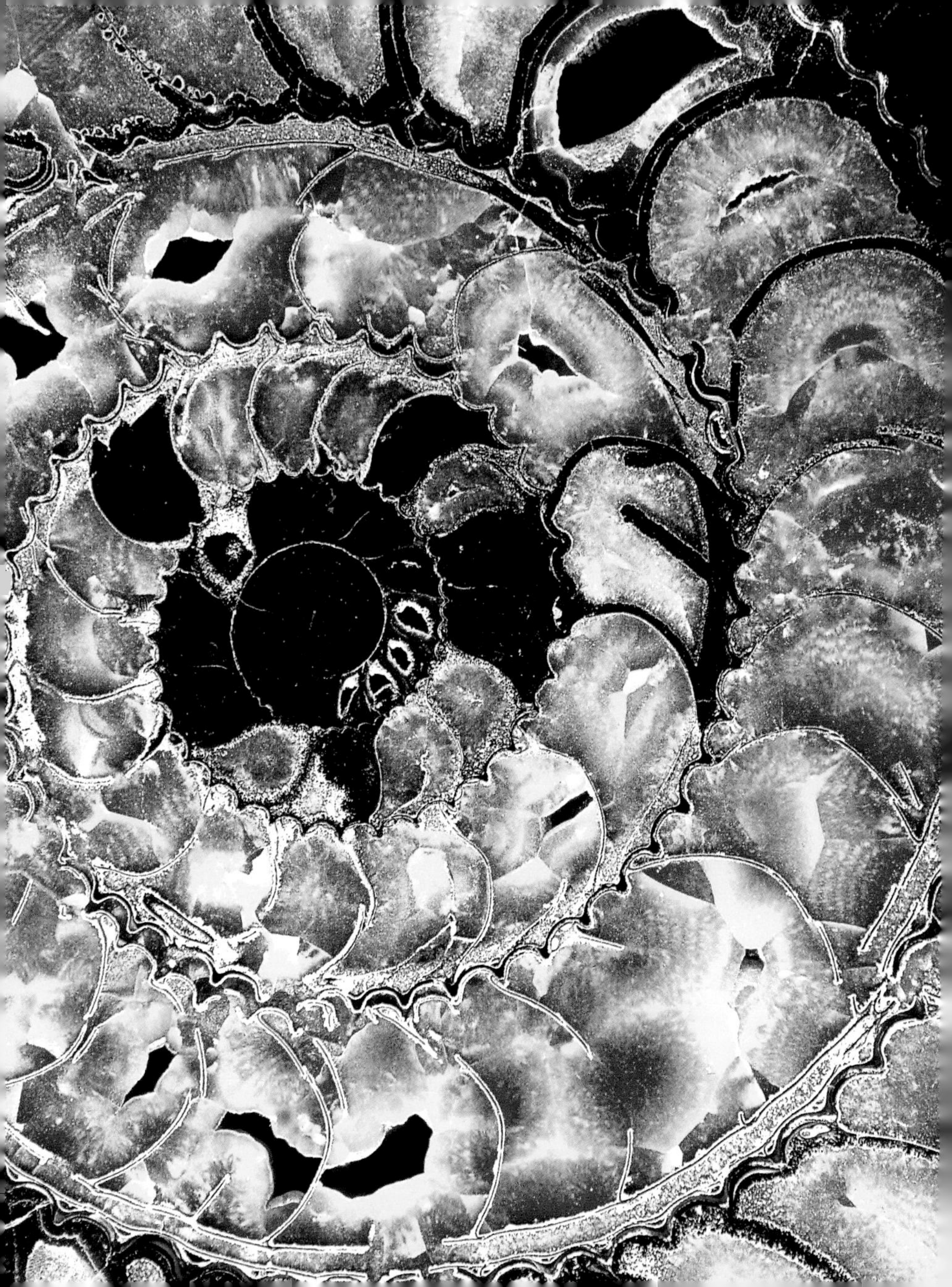

that this stream is constant it is possible to estimate the time the meteorite material took to be deposited by measuring the amount contained in the rock strata.

But how, in practical terms, could he measure the quantity of this material inside rocks that were 65 million years old? Luis and Walter Alvarez decided to measure the quantity of elements that are normally very rare in the rocks that form the earth's crust but which are much more common in certain meteorites. One such element is a metal called iridium. To measure it, Luis and Walter Alvarez called on two geochemistry experts, Frank Asaro and Helen Michel. The results were unexpected, to say the least. In the area around Gubbio, the boundary between the Cretaceous period and the Tertiary is very clearly defined, thanks to the wealth of microfossils present in these marine sediments. It is marked by a narrow layer of dark clay, no more than one centimetre (half an inch) thick, which stands out against the lighter limestone that lies both beneath it (from the Cretaceous period) and above it (from the Tertiary period). In the limestone the iridium content was slight, as is normal in terrestrial rocks. But in the thin clay layer it was much higher: nearly one hundred times more than in the limestone. How could this anomaly be explained? Either the clay layer had taken millions of years to be laid down, which was unlikely, or Earth had received a huge influx of meteorite material at the time it was deposited. This was the theory put forward by the scientists at Berkeley, who published their discovery in 1980 in the journal *Science*.

In this article, which was later to assume historic importance, they explained this iridium anomaly by the impact 65 million years earlier of an enormous meteorite of approximately ten kilometres (six miles) in diameter. In their opinion this impact not only caused a large quantity of iridium (and other rare metals) to be deposited on the surface of the Earth, but also caused the great extinction at the end of the Cretaceous period, bringing about a global ecological disaster. The impact of such an enormous object would have projected enough dust up into the atmosphere to block out the sun and plunge the Earth into darkness for months, with disastrous consequences for many animals.

DINOSAURS WITH A FUTURE

It is amongst this sort of small, carnivorous dinosaur, that palaeontologists are searching for the origin of birds.

In a geological community that had been deeply suspicious of theories of catastrophism for over one hundred and fifty years, this article was bound to give rise to surprise as well as a great deal of scepticism. Proof had to be gathered, therefore, in support of this new theory and several groups of scientists became involved. First of all, it was necessary to establish whether the iridium anomaly of the Cretaceous-Tertiary boundary was a worldwide phenomenon? Research soon confirmed that it was. From Denmark to Tunisia, Canada to New Zealand, including sediment samples taken from the ocean bed, this particular layer of clay was found wherever the boundary between the Cretaceous and the Tertiary periods was preserved in rock strata, and it contained iridium in abnormal quantities.

WHERE DID THE IRIDIUM COME FROM?

Was this iridium really of extraterrestrial origin? Perhaps it was produced by volcanoes, for example, or from some little known sedimentary phenomenon? Additional proof of the impact was needed. After further investigation, it soon transpired that this clay layer did contain additional evidence of an event that was not terrestrial in origin.

One of the significant finds were some minute glassy spheres, thought to be drops of molten rock created by the violence of the impact and projected very great distances, as is known to occur when large meteorites collide with the Earth.

Grains of minerals such as quartz were also found, showing very specific types of deformation in their crystalline structure. These deformations would have been caused by very high, but very brief, pressure. The only natural phenomenon that can produce such shocked quartz, as it is known, is a meteorite impact, and these deformed grains of mineral are widely found in impact craters.

Finally, remains of the meteorite itself were also found, in the form of large numbers of minuscule crystals of nickel-rich magnetic minerals known as nickel spinels. We know that these crystals only form in very specific conditions – when the surface of a meteorite oxidises by 'burning' on entering the atmosphere – so the spinels testified to an enormous meteorite entering the atmosphere at exactly the time under consideration.

THE TELLTALE LAYER

This thin layer of dark clay, separating the Cretaceous period from the Tertiary, contains chemical and mineral proof of the impact of a huge meteorite.

A COMPETING THEORY: VOLCANIC ACTIVITY

It is quite normal in scientific research to put forward competing theories to explain the same phenomenon – after all, confronting the facts helps a decision to be made. To explain this iridium anomaly several scientists, including Vincent Courtillot of the Global Physics Institute in Paris, turned to volcanic activity. Underlying this theory is an undeniable fact: some volcanoes, like the Kilauea in Hawaii, or the Piton de la Fournaise in Reunion, bring abnormally high levels of iridium to the surface. These are volcanoes of a very particular type, called 'hot points', where molten materials from the depths of the Earth's mantle rise up to the surface. Is it possible that the iridium in question came from the depths of the Earth rather than from deepest space? The Deccan Traps, in India, immense basaltic lava flows covering vast areas and reaching huge depths, support this theory (see also page 84). They point to a volcanic

phenomenon of considerable size and, according to modern dating, they were deposited at the end of the Cretaceous period and the beginning of the Tertiary period, straddling the boundary between the two. Rather than seeking the source of the iridium in space, should we not be asking whether it was thrown up by the volcanic activity of the Deccan? And could the worldwide environmental upheavals that were responsible for the end of the dinosaurs have been caused by what was ejected during this period of intense volcanic activity? It is an attractive theory, but does not explain certain facts.

Volcanic activity cannot produce shocked quartz or nickel spinels, the clear signs of a meteorite impact. Furthermore, the Deccan lava flows are not rich in iridium, and a thick layer of this metal has been found in sedimentary rocks lying in between the lava flows, which proves that the iridium was not deposited by any volcanic eruption. Finally, the volcanic activity in the Deccan was not of the explosive type that would have had effects on a global scale. It lasted at least a million years, whereas the extinctions seem to have been sudden and violent.

Could these Deccan eruptions, nevertheless, have had a harmful long-term effect on the world's environment? Some scientists still think so, and regard the combination of the eruptions and the impact as the explanation of this particular mass extinction. For many scientists, however, the disaster caused by the impact is more than adequate to account for the disappearance of a species.

THE SEARCH FOR A CRATER

UNUSUAL CRYSTALS

The visible layers inside this grain of quartz are a result of the enormous pressure created by the impact of a large meteorite.

For supporters of the impact theory, one piece of the puzzle, and a highly significant one at that, was missing, namely the crater. A huge meteorite colliding with the surface of the Earth at great speed explodes, forming a crater. Estimates put the diameter of this type of crater at approximately 20 times that of the meteorite itself. An object about ten kilometres (six miles) in diameter, which is thought to be the size of the meteorite of the Cretaceous-Tertiary boundary incident, must have left a huge crater about 200 kilometres (125 miles) wide on the surface of the Earth, and could hardly pass unnoticed. About one hundred and fifty impact craters of a variety of sizes and ages have been identified. Admittedly, the older they are the more difficult they are to pinpoint, since the outlines have long since been eroded and they have filled up with sediment, but in spite of this, craters have been detected that were formed much more than 65 million years ago. So where was the huge crater that was left behind after the meteorite impact?

This question was much in the minds of scientists during the 1980s, but it wasn't until the beginning of the 1990s that they first started to believe that they might have stumbled across the crater they had sought for so long. It was situated on the northern coast of the Yucatan peninsula in Mexico, straddling the continent and the Gulf of Mexico. However, as so much time had passed, it was no longer visible as part of the landscape. This meant that a lot of research was necessary in order to see if their theories could be confirmed.

Oil drilling in the area around 1960, revealed a curious geological structure in the depths of the earth, but at the time, this was held to be of volcanic origin. In the 1990s geophysical techniques were used to explore this mysterious structure, which scientists were now beginning to suspect was an impact crater. By noting the variations in the earth's magnetic field as well as those of gravity in the region, it was possible to obtain fairly precise images of the buried structure. The form of a crater soon became evident, with a diameter of at least 200 kilometres (125 miles), and showing many concentric ridges – a typical feature of large impact craters. By looking closely at core samples, scientists were able to confirm that at the bottom of the crater, under the sediment that had filled it in, were the characteristic crushed and molten rocks. The crater was, therefore, definitely the result of an impact. The dating carried out on the molten rock at the bottom of the crater indicated an age of 65 million years, so the dimensions and the age fitted the theory. It was also possible to show that certain minerals found in the clay strata of the same period, in the west of the United States, came from the Mexican crater. In addition to this, all around the Gulf of Mexico, the deposits of the Cretaceous-Tertiary boundary period showed traces of upheavals, including an enormous tidal wave.

METEORITE CRATER

In Arizona, 50,000 years ago, a meteorite carved out this spectacular impact crater, measuring 1,200 metres (3,900 feet) across and 200 metres (660 feet) deep.

Most scientists today are convinced by this theory; the Chicxulub crater – the name taken from a village located near its centre – is quite definitely the legacy of an enormous 65 million year old meteorite collision.

THE EXTINCTION SCENARIO

However, even if the fact of the impact is no longer in doubt, we still need to understand how it could have caused a mass extinction. Based on the estimated mass of the meteorite and its speed, we can calculate the energy released at the time of the collision. In the case of Chicxulub, it is estimated that this energy was equivalent to five billion times that of the atomic bomb dropped on Hiroshima in 1945, so it is not difficult to imagine the large-scale devastation that such an explosion would have caused. However, this particular extinction was worldwide, and we know that dinosaurs in Australia, for example, were not immediately

wiped out by the direct effects of the Yucatan impact. Rather than immediate destruction on a local or regional scale, it is the more long-term, indirect consequences –this time on a global scale – that we need to look at.

Many extinction scenarios have been suggested since 1980. Some exaggerate: they depict an Earth transformed into a virtual hell, a furnace which would have eliminated all life – something that was clearly not the case. Nevertheless, the consequences of the impact were catastrophic for large numbers of living creatures, not just dinosaurs.

The main responsibility for the disaster rests, without doubt, on the enormous quantity of dust produced by the collision. Under the violence of the collision, the meteorite and rocks at the point of impact would have been vaporised, forming a gigantic ball of fire. Then the dust that was created, which would have contained huge quantities of iridium, would have spread up into the atmosphere, forming an immense cloud covering the Earth, so thick that the Earth would have been plunged into darkness. It is estimated that it was several months before this dust slowly fell back to the surface of the planet, to form its telltale layer.

THE FATAL INSTANT

It was the knock-on consequences of the impact, rather than the immediate effects, that ultimately proved fatal to the dinosaurs.

THE EARTH IS PLUNGED INTO DARKNESS

During this long period the plant world was severely affected by the lack of light. Green plants use sunlight for photosynthesis, the process which allows them to use the carbon dioxide in the atmosphere for growth. The first consequence of the period of darkness would have been a general withering of vegetation, and traces of this effect can be found in the rocks of the time. In the deposits of very old lakes in the American West, for example, at the same level where iridium enrichment testifies to the impact, the quantity of pollen grains contained in the sediment decreases spectacularly, while that of fern spores increases. We interpret this as indicating a temporary withering of pollen-producing flowers and a recolonisation by ferns, always the first plants to re-occupy devastated areas. Once the dust had dispersed and light was able to get through again, plants were obviously able to regrow from seeds, spores, and rhizomes, as they always do once adverse conditions come to an end. Many animals, however, were not able to survive this period of acute crisis, because the death of the plants brought about a crucial break in their food chains.

In order to survive, the herbivorous dinosaurs needed large quantities of fresh plants. It would not be surprising, therefore, if they died of starvation when this crucial food source was denied to them over several months. At the other extreme, the carnivorous dinosaurs that preyed on herbivorous dinosaurs were also deprived of their food and died as a result.

In the seas there was a similar scenario. Plant plankton depends as much on photosynthesis as land-based plants, and the period of darkness would inevitably have led to a break in a food chain that linked together animal plankton, ammonites and belemnites, and ended with the plesiosaurs and the mosasaurs, which all disappeared. However, explaining the disappearances is one thing; we also need to understand how certain animals were able to survive the disaster. Here too, the key to the mystery is to be found in the food chains. Not all organisms depended, at least in the short term, on living plants. In the seas, for example, those that lived on the sea bed found their food by filtering small particles of organic matter from the silt. Such communities would have been able to survive for some time, although the lack of light was fatal to planktonic surface plants and animals and all those that fed on them. This, in effect, is what the fossils tell us: the animals living on the ocean floor survived better than those that floated or swam closer to the surface of the water.

MASSACRE IN THE OCEANS

Only a few fresh-water animals, however, became extinct at the end of the Cretaceous period. This aquatic community included small invertebrates which fed off organic particles suspended in the water, rather than living plants, and they in turn were eaten by fish or amphibians, which in turn acted as prey for freshwater turtles and crocodiles. The survival of all these animals, therefore, can be explained by the survival of the food chain to which they belonged during the critical period of darkness.

Finally, how was it possible that numbers of small land animals also survived, such as lizards, snakes and mammals? The answer is that these sorts of animals fed on insects and worms which found their food in the organic matter contained in the soil and humus, and so were not reliant on sunlight-loving plant life. Therefore there was a food chain, albeit a reduced one, that was able to survive.

PLANT FOSSILS

Despite the extremely adverse conditions that followed the impact of the meteorite, most plants, like the maidenhair tree – whose leaves are shown here – survived.

This theory of the fates of different food chains provides a very satisfactory explanation for the extinctions and survivals that can be observed at the Cretaceous-Tertiary boundary. Some questions though, continue to baffle palaeontologists: Why were the small, carnivorous dinosaurs not able to survive by eating the smaller land animals that did not perish? What exactly happened to the birds, which are descended from dinosaurs? They were numerous at the end of the Cretaceous period, they certainly survived the crisis and underwent considerable development in the Tertiary period, but did they nevertheless suffer a severe reduction in numbers at the Cretaceous-Tertiary boundary, as some scientists think? Much work remains to

be done in order to understand the finer details of this mass extinction. We must also not lose sight of the fact that the natural and environmental balance is a fragile one, and a crisis of this magnitude may have had indirect repercussions on many other organisms that were not directly affected by the loss of their food source. The work of biologists on present-day extinctions, chiefly caused by man's actions, show the detailed and complex nature of the problem. To reconstruct in detail an ecological crisis which took place 65 million years ago is a fascinating undertaking, but it is certainly by no means straightforward.

THE RETURN OF CATASTROPHISM

The period of prolonged darkness that was to bring the reign of the dinosaurs to an end could not have gone on for very long. If it had, extinction would have been even more widespread. The fate of the dinosaurs has to be seen as a very brief phenomenon in the geological time-scale, to be viewed in terms, not of millions of years, but of months and years. Many geologists and palaeontologists find this change of time-scale difficult to adjust to, but it is necessary if the idea of a mass extinction due to the impact at Chicxulub is accepted as the likeliest explanation.

We know that Cuvier had not given any special thought to the impact of extraterrestrial objects as a possible cause for his 'global revolutions' (admittedly, in his time the existence of meteorites was only just beginning to be accepted), but the discoveries of modern science proved him right.

Life certainly has been threatened on several occasions, since the mass extinction at the end of the Cretaceous period is not the only one that palaeontologists have discovered, nor is it the most serious. It is estimated, for example, that the great biological crisis that took place 250 million years ago at the boundary between the Permian and the Triassic periods caused the disappearance of almost 90 per cent of living species. Were all these great extinctions caused by the impact of giant meteorites? At the moment we can only guess at the probable causes. The only mass extinctions for which incontrovertible evidence of an impact exists is the one which occurred 65 million years ago – but it is also the only one, so far, that has been studied in such depth.

THE ORIGIN OF BIRDS

Archaeopteryx, the oldest known bird, has a skeleton similar in many respects to those of carnivorous dinosaurs.

Following the discovery of the Chicxulub crater our vision of the history of living creatures can never be the same again. At the end of the Cretaceous period the continents were dominated by huge reptiles – dinosaurs. After the impact of the cataclysmic meteorite there were no land animals left weighing more than 25 kilograms (55 pounds). In the absence of large animals the opportunities for the survivors were greatly increased, benefiting mammals in particular.

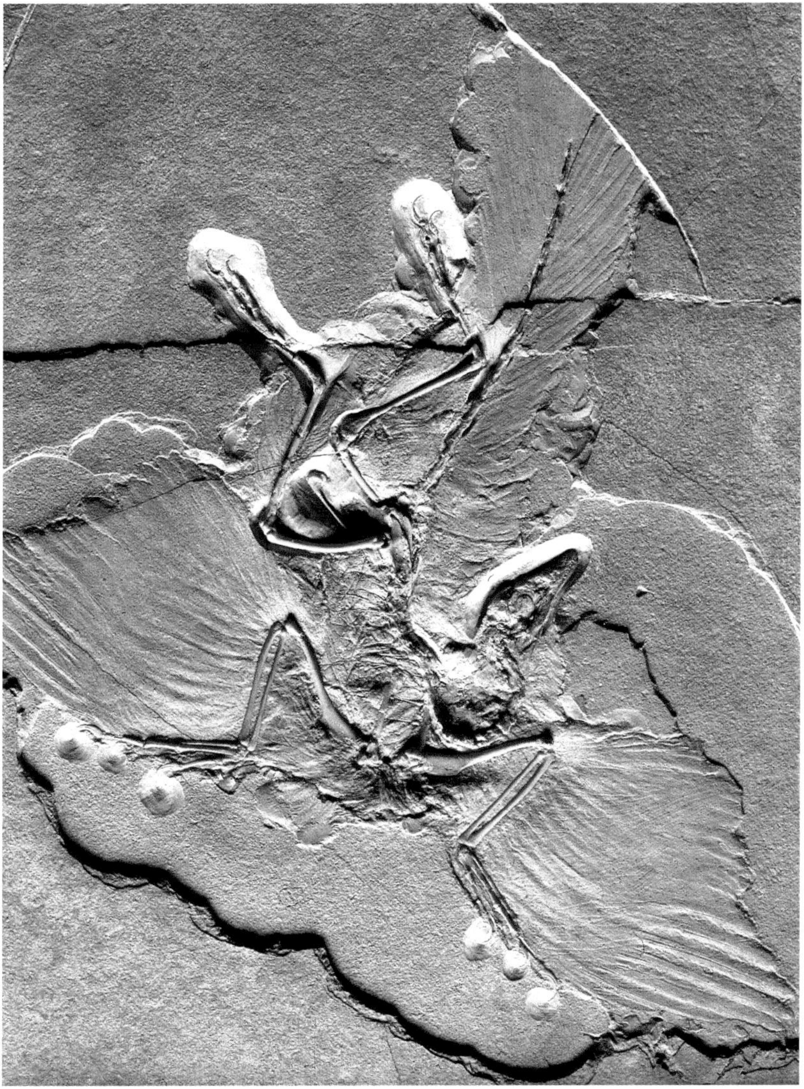

They needed time – a few million years – to diversify, increase in size and adapt to environments they had not occupied during the time of the dinosaurs. The Cenozoic period thus became the era of mammals, including primates, notably one set of invasive primates – humans. When a mass extinction of some sort occurs, what is bad luck for some is good luck for others – and such events can change the face of the world. To a large extent the world we know today is the result of the great catastrophe that took place 65 million years ago.

BAD LUCK OR NATURAL SELECTION?

It was not merely a matter of chance that mammals survived while dinosaurs disappeared. At the time of the catastrophe the diet of some animals allowed them to survive an ecological disaster that others could not. In these exceptional circumstances one particular aspect of natural selection played its part, and certain creatures found that they were better equipped than others in the struggle for existence. Cuvier was not so wrong after all, and Darwin was only partly right.

The theories of catastrophism and evolution are not mutually exclusive, and recent discoveries about the last days of the dinosaurs would tend to encourage us to attempt some kind of marriage between the two theories.

SOME SURVIVORS

Among the animals that survived the aftermath of the meteorite impact are the members of the crocodile family, cousins of the dinosaurs.

The fate of the dinosaurs reminds us that our planet does not enjoy any particular protection in a universe in which violent events can happen. However, the next great extinction – which has already started – has no extraterrestrial origin. Its causes are known, even if all the details aren't fully understood; it is the alteration of the natural environment by humans. Perhaps it is an irony of fate that among the victims are many species of the one animal group which provides us with a link to the dinosaurs of the Mesozoic era, namely birds.

The bone structure of a modern bird clearly shows its links with the past.

Charles Darwin, naturalist.

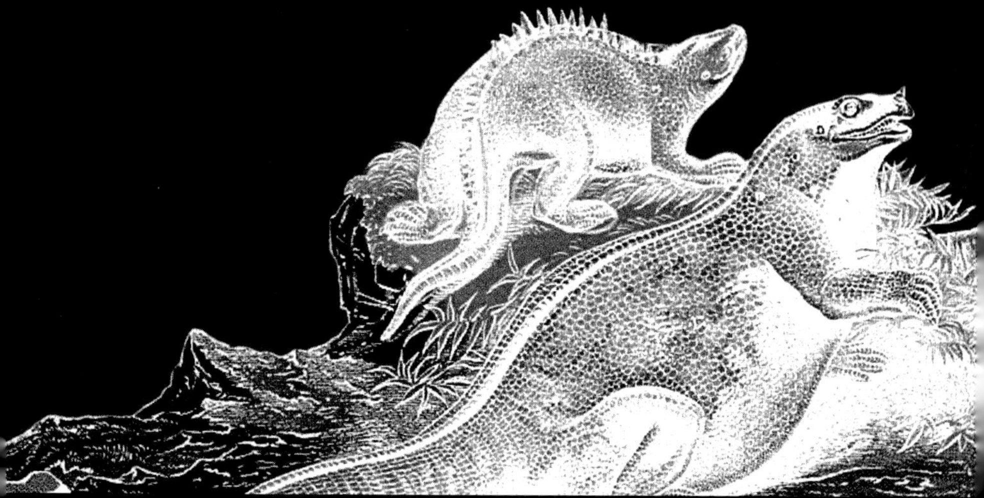

LOOK

FROM THE 19TH CENTURY ONWARDS PALAEONTOLOGISTS REALISED THAT THE DISTANT PAST OF THE EARTH COULD BE DIVIDED UP INTO SUCCESSIVE PERIODS, CHARACTERISED BY THEIR FAUNA AND FLORA, AND OFTEN SEPARATED BY GREAT EXTINCTIONS. THE RECONSTRUCTION OF THIS SEQUENCE OF PERIODS WAS A CHALLENGE THAT BROUGHT TOGETHER ARTISTS AND SCIENTISTS.

The Carboniferous, a heavily forested period from which most of our coal deposits date

is also the time of the first reptiles. They lived on the edges of vast swamps.

but some also left the land to become dominant in the sea.

Reptiles triumphed on land and in water in the Jurassic period. The first birds, probably the best known of which

was Archaeopteryx, shared the mastery of the air with the flying reptiles, the pterosaurs.

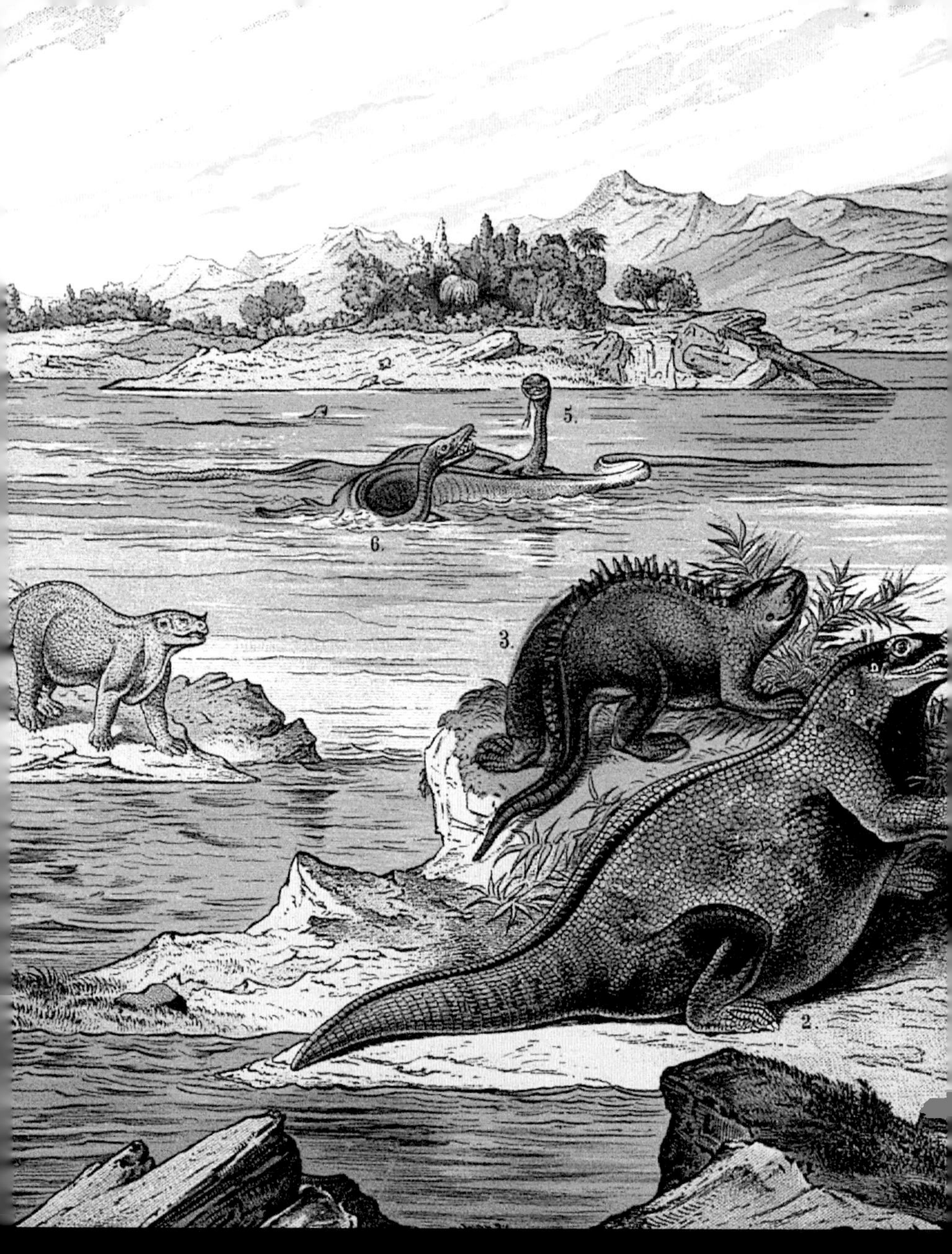

Dinosaurs reached their peak in the Cretaceous period and then disappeared. These 19th-century depictions

show how much our ideas of dinosaurs have changed over the last hundred years or so.

In the Tertiary period, after the dinosaurs became extinct, mammals started to flourish.

However millions of years were to pass before they reached the sizes of the animals shown in this illustration

Ice ages and the appearance of man were features of the Quaternary period.

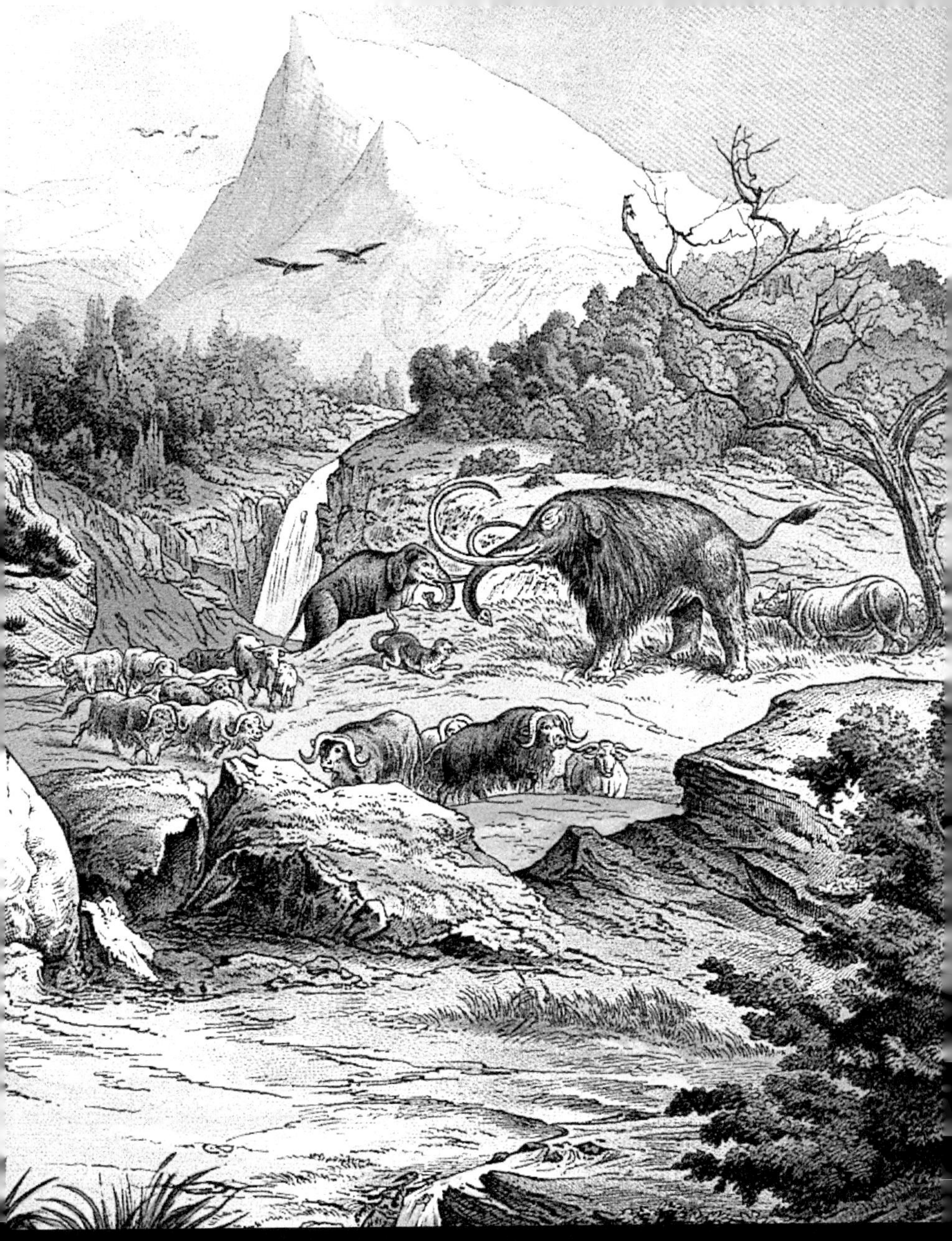

This illustration shows the caveman of common myth defending his cave against the attack of a dangerous bear

The cover of the 1886 German publication from which these illustrations of the six geological ages have been taken

IN PRACTICE

WHO WERE THE LAST DINOSAURS AND WHAT DO WE REALLY KNOW ABOUT THEM? THE MAIN EXTINCTION THEORIES. THE RECONSTRUCTION OF AN ASTEROID IMPACT. THE CRATER AT CHICXULUB. OTHER VICTIMS OF THE CRISIS AND SOME OF THE SURVIVORS. THE DESCENDANTS OF THE DINOSAURS.

What is a dinosaur?

In spite of British palaeontologist Richard Owen calling them 'terrible lizards', dinosaurs were only distantly related to lizards; more accurately, they are extinct reptiles, with a characteristic limb skeleton and method of movement.

Reptiles that didn't crawl

Present-day reptiles, such as crocodiles or lizards, usually move by crawling, their limbs set at the sides, with the main part of their body and tail dragging on the ground. Dinosaurs, on the other hand, held their bodies off the ground, with legs tucked underneath, as is evident from the shape of the bones in their limbs and their pelvis. This allowed efficient back and forward leg movements which may have been the key to their success.

Bipeds or quadrupeds?

Some dinosaurs were bipeds (ie they walked mainly on their two hind legs) while others were quadrupeds, using all four legs equally; some undoubtedly used both types of stance. Dinosaurs were strictly land animals; the flying reptiles and sea reptiles that were their contemporaries were not dinosaurs.

THE ORNITHISCHIAN GROUP
dinosaurs with a four-branched bird-like pelvis (eg Triceratops).

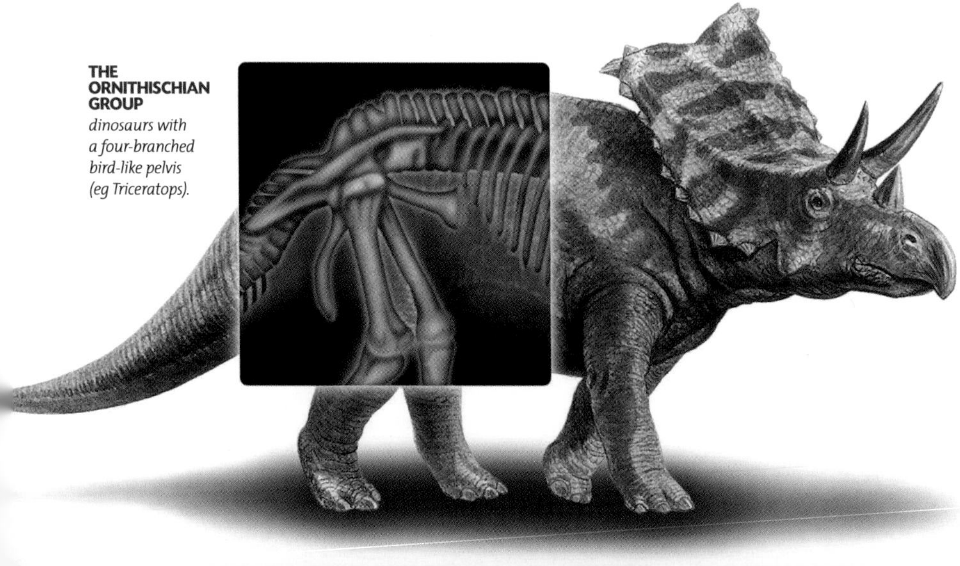

An unparelleled reign

Dinosaurs appeared about 230 million years ago, during the Triassic period. Their long evolution subsequently spread over the Jurassic and Cretaceous periods, lasting a total of 165 million years.

Two large groups of dinosaurs

Dinosaurs are divided into two main groups, depending on the structure of their pelvis. The Saurischia (dinosaurs with a lizard-like pelvis) with three branches. The Ornithischia (dinosaurs with a bird-like pelvis) had one with four branches.

OVER EIGHT HUNDRED SPECIES IDENTIFIED

To date palaeontologists have catalogued more than eight hundred species of dinosaur. When you consider that this is a group of animals that was at large for around 165 million years, it is likely that so far only a small percentage of the different types of dinosaur that actually existed have been found.

Their diet

The main evidence for our knowledge on this subject comes from the shape of their teeth. Among the Saurischia, we know there were both carnivorous and herbivorous species, whereas all the Ornithischia were herbivorous.

THE SAURISCHIAN GROUP
dinosaurs with a three-branched lizard-like pelvis (eg Tyrannosaurus).

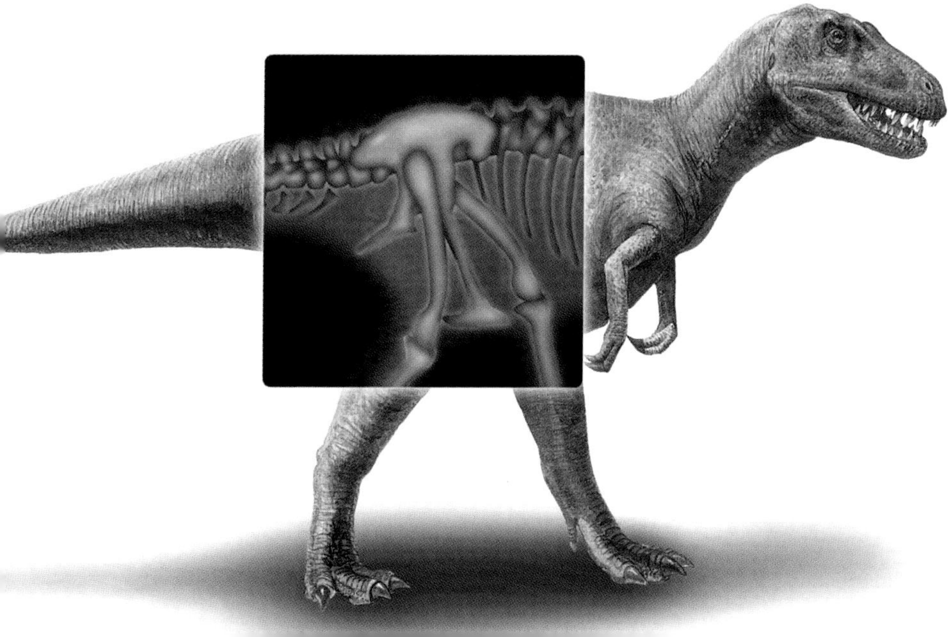

Footprints, eggs, fossils – on the trail of a dinosaur

The only knowledge we have of dinosaurs derives from the fossils left behind in rocks. More often than not these are skeletal remains, but footprints, eggs and – more rarely – remains of skin or internal organs, and even droppings, have been found.

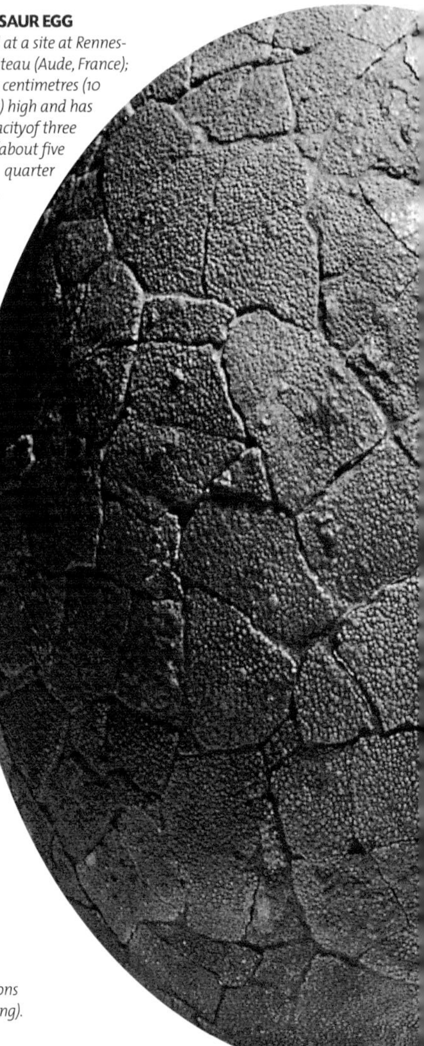

DINOSAUR EGG
Found at a site at Rennes-le-Château (Aude, France); it is 25 centimetres (10 inches) high and has a capacityof three litres (about five and a quarter pints).

The discovery of a site

This usually happens by accident (for example, discovering remains while carrying out other work) or, alternatively, by methodical digging with the aim of finding fossils. Palaeontologists uncovering a site containing the remains of dinosaurs use tried and tested techniques that enable them to extract fossils in the best possible condition. These techniques ensure that the palaeontologists can gather the maximum amount of information about the fossils and prevent any damage during transportation to the laboratory. There the fossils are prepared and made available for scientific study and subsequent exhibition to the public.

FOSSILISED DINOSAUR TEETH
found during excavations (2–3cm/about 1 inch long).

In the field

Having established the approximate overall shape of a bone, the surrounding rock needs to be cut away to leave a block. This is then wrapped in a shell of paper and strips of cloth soaked in plaster which, once they have hardened, make it possible to remove the entire block and transport it without breaking or disturbing the fossil inside.

Investigation

The real scientific investigation starts in the field, with a detailed note being made of the position of the bones, in order to record how they are arranged on the site, and the types of rock that surround them.

PRECISION WORK

The final extraction of the bone is carried out using whatever method is most appropriate (either removing the remaining surrounding rock using small implements, or dissolving it with acid, etc.). Once laboratory preparation is complete, each bone is described, measured and analysed in order to identify the animal as precisely as possible and to determine whether it is a new species.

BONES

These are carefully extracted from their rocky surroundings; depending on how hard this is, the tools could range from a pick hammer to a needle.

MAKING A CAST

Generally, specimens have to be stabilised by impregnating them with resins that harden as they dry.

FOOTPRINT

The footprint of a dinosaur found in Thailand.

Where do you find them?

This map of the main sites at which dinosaur fossils have been found shows that the remains of these animals have been discovered from the equator to the poles.

Hotter climates

Dinosaurs inhabited all of the continents, although at that time the continents were not in the position they currently occupy and the climates were quite different from what they are nowadays.

Research

The countries where particularly large numbers of dinosaur remains have been found include the United States, Canada, China, Mongolia, Argentina and Tanzania. However, all the regions of the world have not been investigated with equal thoroughness and new sites are discovered every year. Even in areas that one might think had been thoroughly explored, like Europe, there are frequent discoveries of new species of dinosaur. Nevertheless, sites containing remains of the very last dinosaurs – those that lived at the extreme end of the Cretaceous period just before their final demise – are still relatively few, and are located mainly in the west of North America, southern Europe and China.

The first finds

The first dinosaur fossils to be studied scientifically came from western Europe and, in particular, from England.

CRETACEOUS ○

JURASSIC ●

TRIASSIC ●

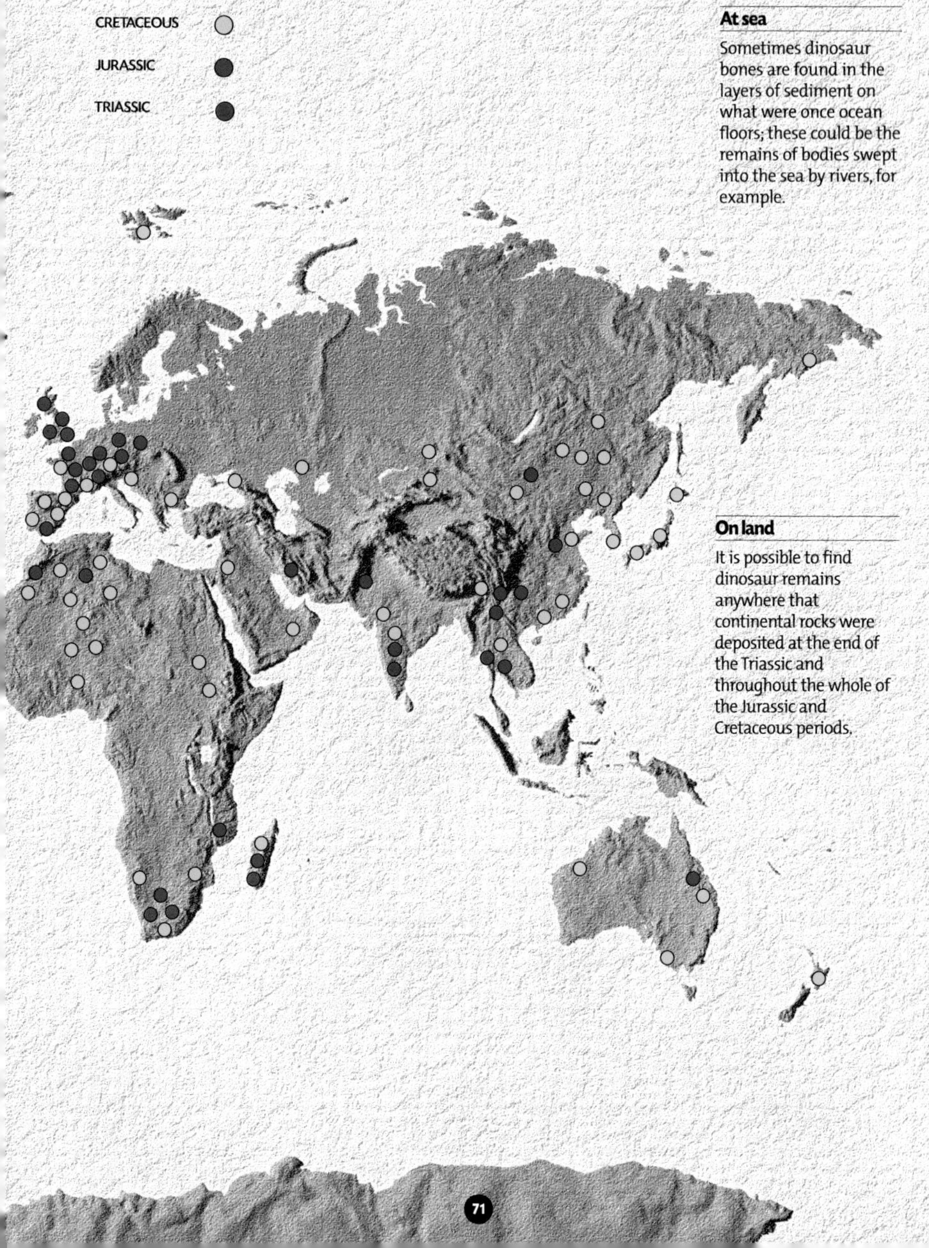

At sea

Sometimes dinosaur bones are found in the layers of sediment on what were once ocean floors; these could be the remains of bodies swept into the sea by rivers, for example.

On land

It is possible to find dinosaur remains anywhere that continental rocks were deposited at the end of the Triassic and throughout the whole of the Jurassic and Cretaceous periods.

Who were the last dinosaurs?

Dinosaur remains from the end of the Cretaceous period – ie the period preceding their final disappearance – have been found all over the world. Some types of dinosaur were common to several regions, but others were not, and by the final millions of years of the Cretaceous period many different types of dinosaur had developed worldwide. The dinosaurs illustrated on the following pages came from the west of Canada and the United States, where some very prolific deposits have yielded large numbers of skeletons.

SAURISCHIAN DASPLETOSAURUS, TYRANNOSAURIDAE

Length: 8.50 metres (28 feet). This member of the Tyrannosaur family was not as big as the famous Tyrannosaurus, which was 12 metres (39 feet) long, but it was nevertheless a very respectably-sized carnivore, capable of attacking large plant-eating dinosaurs. Its forelimbs were very small, and its main weapons were its powerful jaws armed with a large number of strong, sharp teeth.

SAURISCHIAN DROMAEOSAURUS, DROMAEOSAURIDAE

Length: 1.80 metres (6 feet). This small carnivorous dromaeosaur (or 'running dinosaur') belonged to a family related to the predecessors of birds. It was armed with sharp teeth and powerful claws, which made it a formidable predator, perhaps even capable of attacking animals considerably larger than itself. Each foot had a well-developed claw that could be used to disembowel its prey.

SAURISCHIAN ORNITHOMIMUS, ORNITHOMIMIDAE

Length: 3.50 metres (almost 10 feet). This dinosaur belongs to a family often called 'ostrich-dinosaurs' because they resemble these large, running birds. This similarity is all the more marked because they do not have teeth and their jaw is almost like a beak. Like ostriches, these dinosaurs had to be able to run fast. Their diet remains a mystery but in all likelihood they were vegetarian.

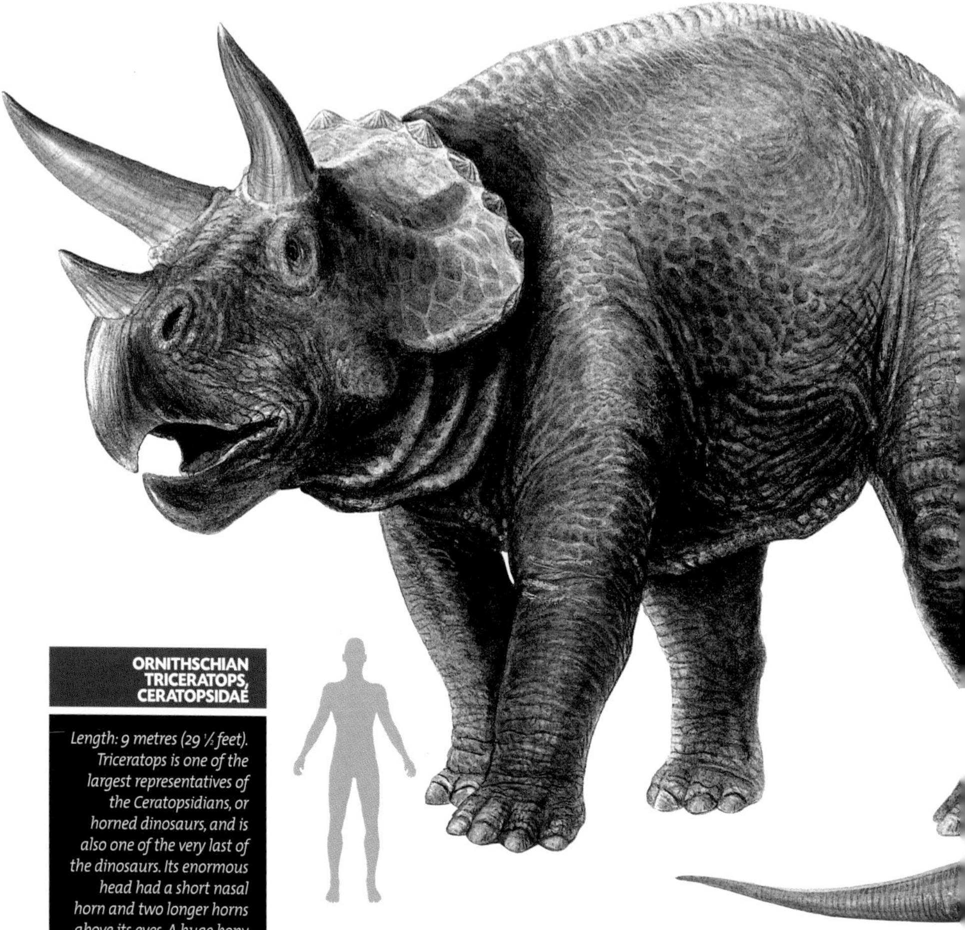

ORNITHSCHIAN TRICERATOPS, CERATOPSIDAE

Length: 9 metres (29 ½ feet). Triceratops is one of the largest representatives of the Ceratopsidians, or horned dinosaurs, and is also one of the very last of the dinosaurs. Its enormous head had a short nasal horn and two longer horns above its eyes. A huge bony collar covered the back of its neck. Its jaws ended in a toothless beak, but further back it had a number of teeth suitable for grinding plant food.

ORNITHISCHIAN ANKYLOSAURUS, ANKYLOSAURIDAE

Length: 10 metres (33 feet). The Ankylosaurs were armoured dinosaurs whose bodies were covered by a powerful armour of scales and bony spikes, from their heads to the ends of their tails. The tail ended in a bony club that the animals could use to hit their attackers. This impressive defence system made it possible for plant-eaters with very small teeth to protect themselves against meat-eating dinosaurs.

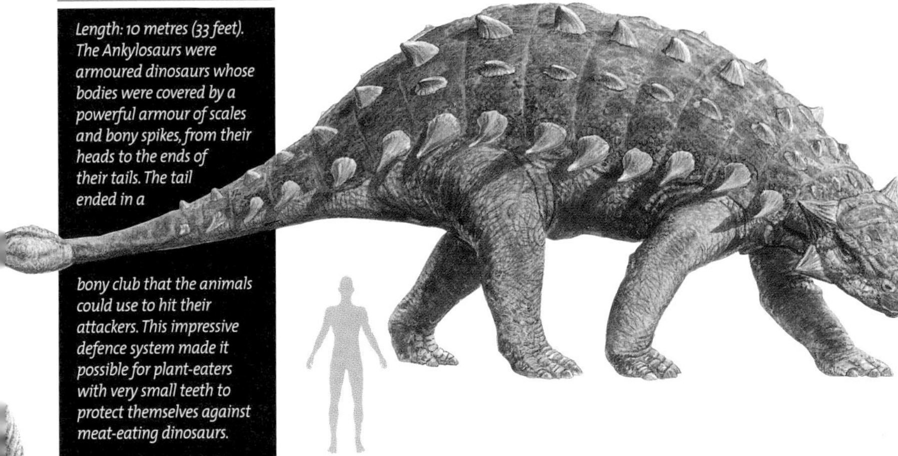

ORNITHISCHIAN ANATOTITAN, HADROSAURIDAE

Length: 10 metres (33 feet). This is a typical example of the hadrosaurs, or duck-billed dinosaurs. The front part of the jaw was, in fact, flat and toothless. To compensate for this they were provided with a large number of teeth set further back and arranged in groups, which were capable of grinding up tough plants. These dinosaurs were able to adopt a two or four-legged stance at will, and some of them seem to have lived in herds.

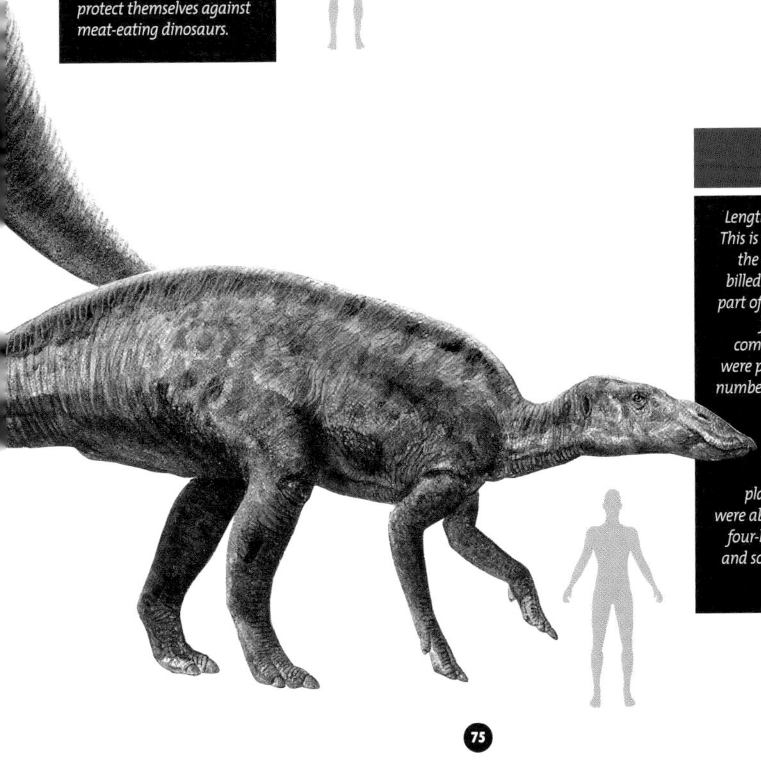

How much do we really know about dinosaurs?

However realistic the reconstruction of a dinosaur may seem, it must always be remembered that it is based on fossil remains – essentially bones – and, in rare cases, traces of skin and tracks. On the basis of these sorts of clues palaeontologists can suggest a reconstruction, like this one of the Tsintaosaurus spinorhinus, a duck-billed dinosaur (hadrosaur), found in China and dating from some 70 million years ago.

THE SKIN

We know about the skin texture of some dinosaurs, such as the Tsintaosaurus and other related species, because tracks have been found which suggest they had a sort of thick leather that was studded with little bumps. Other dinosaurs had very different skin; certain small theropods even show evidence of feathers. The colours, though, are pure guesswork.

THE TAIL

From the tracks of these dinosaurs, and the absence of any furrow that would otherwise have been left, it has been deduced that the tail was held above ground.

THE HEAD

The projection on the forehead of the Tsintaosaurus is a hollow tube formed by nasal bones. The theory is that these tubes, found on the skulls of various hadrosaurs, could be filled with air, allowing the animals to make sounds that were part of their social behaviour.

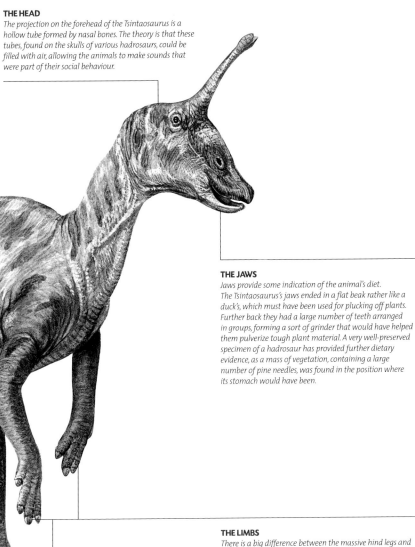

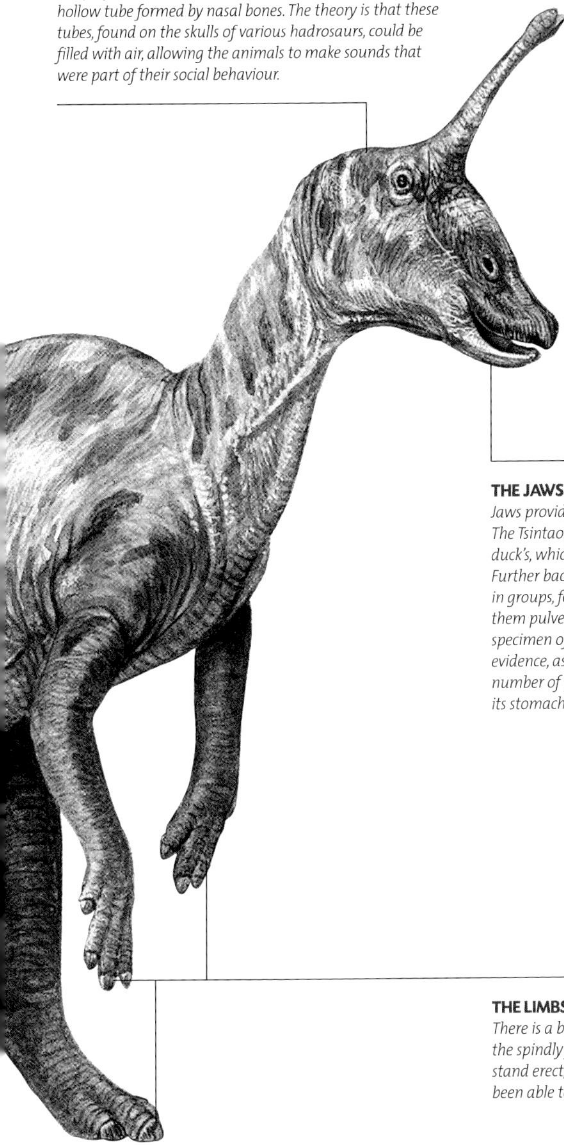

THE JAWS

Jaws provide some indication of the animal's diet. The Tsintaosaurus's jaws ended in a flat beak rather like a duck's, which must have been used for plucking off plants. Further back they had a large number of teeth arranged in groups, forming a sort of grinder that would have helped them pulverize tough plant material. A very well-preserved specimen of a hadrosaur has provided further dietary evidence, as a mass of vegetation, containing a large number of pine needles, was found in the position where its stomach would have been.

THE LIMBS

There is a big difference between the massive hind legs and the spindly front legs. This suggests that Tsintaosaurus could stand erect, as in this reconstruction, but it must also have been able to stand on all fours when required.

The end of the dinosaurs – their place in Earth's history

Although millions of years have passed since dinosaurs last walked the Earth, it isn't really that long ago when compared to the age of the Earth itself, which is approximately 4.5 billion years. The great crisis which caused, among other things, the disappearance of the dinosaurs, marks the boundary between two of the great eras that make up the major divisions of geological time, the Mesozoic era (from 250 to 65 million years ago) and the Cenozoic era (which began 65 million years ago).

The Mesozoic

Following the Palaeozoic, or the age of ancient life (from 540 to 250 million years ago), the Mesozoic, or the age of middle life, is characterised by the large number of reptiles (including dinosaurs) that roamed the earth at this time.

The Cenozoic

This geological era is often called the 'Age of Mammals' because of their proliferation after the dinosaurs became extinct.

The Cretaceous-Tertiary boundary

Another term used is the K-T boundary – the letter 'K' coming from the German kreide (chalk). To be precise, this boundary corresponds to the division between the geological age known as Maastrichtian (after the town of Maastricht, in Holland, where the rocks from this era are easily visible), the last age of the Cretaceous and the Danian Age (after Denmark), the first part of the Palaeocene period, which marks the beginning of the Tertiary period.

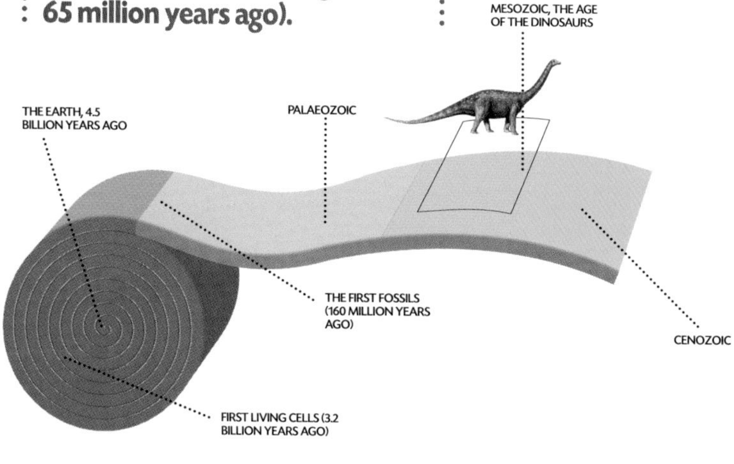

The rings in this diagram make it possible to chart precisely the period marking the disappearance of the dinosaurs against the calendar of the Earth's history.

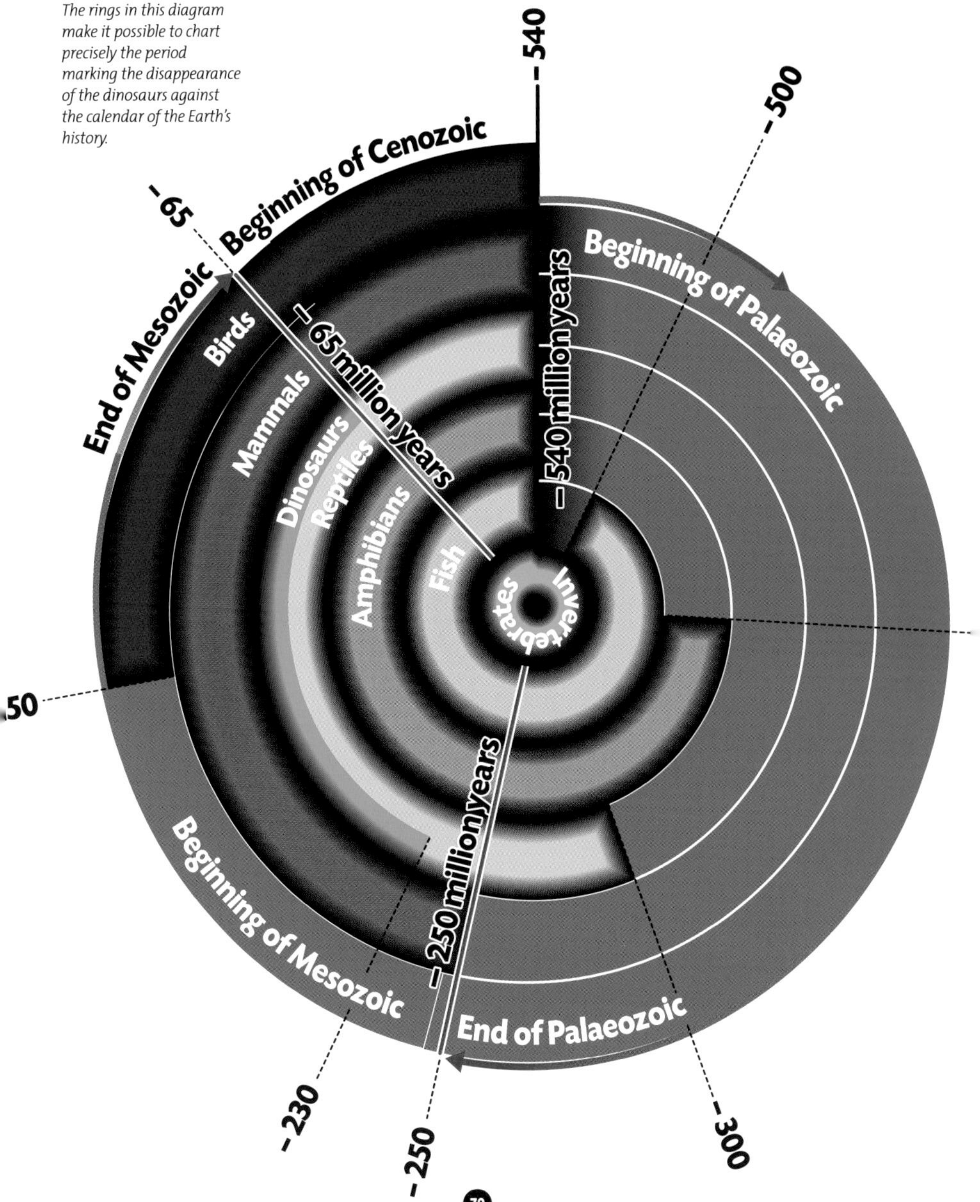

Plate tectonics and continental drift – evolution speeds up

JURASSIC

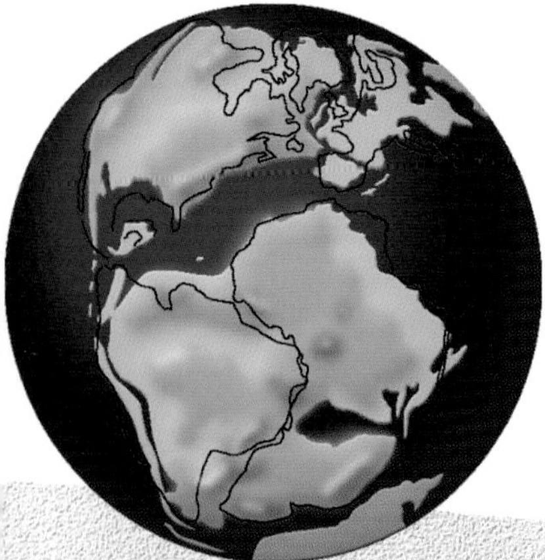

Between the appearance and disappearance of the dinosaurs 165 million years passed, during which time the surface of the globe altered quite considerably under the effect of the forces of plate tectonics. This fragmentation of the world's continents explains the great diversity amongst the last dinosaurs.

The break-up of Pangaea

When the dinosaurs first appeared, in the Triassic, the continents were all joined together in a land mass known as Pangaea. From the beginning of the Jurassic period this began to break up, first into two supercontinents, one in the South – Gondwana – the other in the North – Laurasia. These in turn broke up as new

oceans opened up, producing the separate continents that we know today.

Continental drift

At the end of the Cretaceous period the continents had already moved apart. The Southern Atlantic Ocean was developing, separating Africa from South America. The Northern Atlantic had also begun to develop, starting to isolate Europe from North America. Africa was separated from Europe by a sea known as Tethys.

Sea levels

A further factor that influenced the geography at the end of the Cretaceous period was the high sea level. Many of today's land areas were covered by water at the time, and Europe, separated from Asia by a narrow stretch of sea in the area of the Urals, consisted of an archipelago of different-sized islands.

Climates

Climates were generally hotter than they are today, and there were no polar ice caps. All the same, the study of plant fossils shows that there were climatic differences, with more temperate conditions in the Arctic and Antarctic regions. Once the continents separated, the fauna of each were able to evolve in reasonably isolated conditions for millions of years, and thus became clearly differentiated from each other.

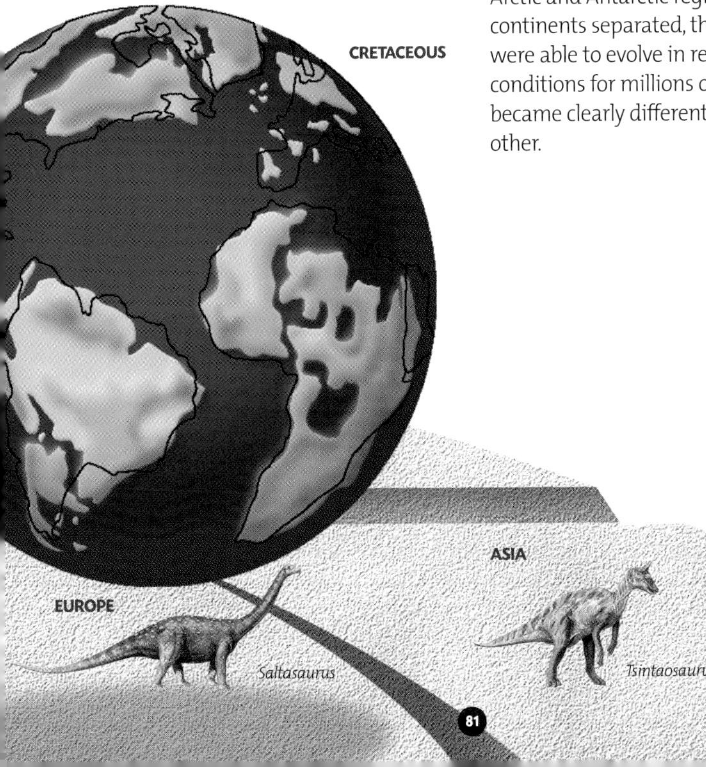

REFERENCE POINTS

During the Cenozoic, after the disappearance of the dinosaurs, the land masses and the oceans slowly took on the positions they have today.

Other victims of the disaster

Dinosaurs were not the only living creatures to disappear so abruptly. It is estimated that 70 per cent of the species living at the very end of the Cretaceous disappeared during the mass extinction.

MARINE PLANKTON

Although many groups of creatures were annihilated at the Cretaceous-Tertiary boundary there were others that did survive, even though their numbers were cut drastically. This was particularly the case with marine plankton: the quantity and types were massively reduced, but eventually many new species evolved from the few that remained at the beginning of the Tertiary period.

CARNIVOROUS MARINE REPTILES

Two groups that lived in the open sea in the late Cretaceous period disappeared at the time of the Cretaceous-Tertiary boundary: mosasaurs, giant lizards adapted to living in water, and the plesiosaurs, many of which had small heads and long necks.

ELASMOSAURUS

Rudists

These very unusual bivalve molluscs formed reefs in shallow seas during the Cretaceous period. At the end of the Cretaceous they disappeared.

PTEROSAURS

These flying reptiles, that had wings consisting of a membrane stretched from one digit at the end of a very long arm to their back leg, appeared in the Triassic period, like the dinosaurs, and diversified throughout the Jurassic and the Cretaceous periods. Ultimately, a number of giant species developed, attaining a wingspan of about 10 metres (33 feet). They too were victims of the mass extinction at the Cretaceous-Tertiary boundary.

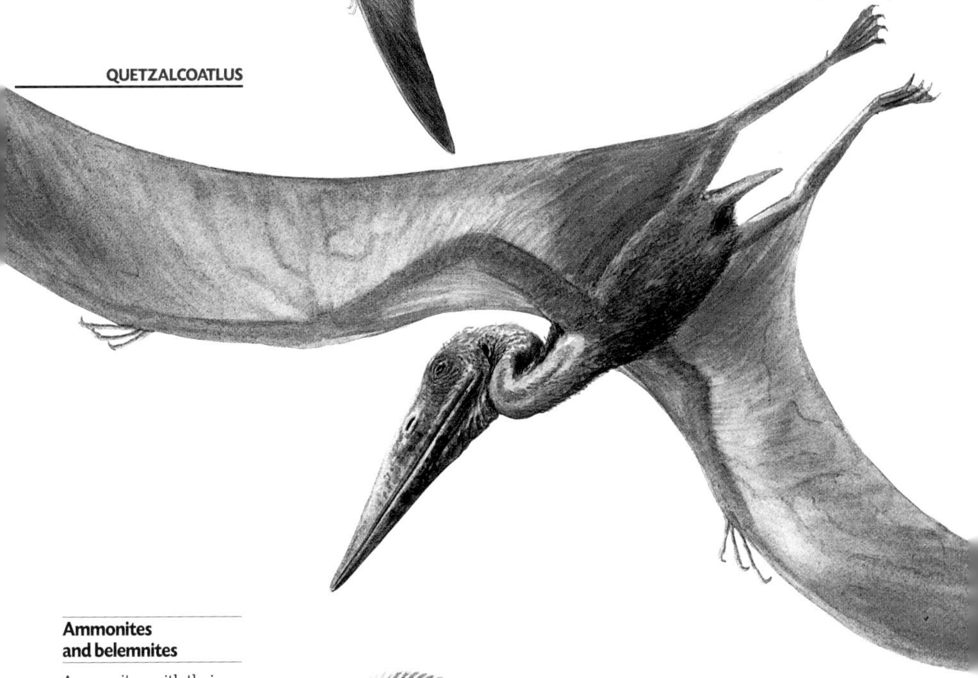

QUETZALCOATLUS

Ammonites and belemnites

Ammonites, with their spiral shells, and belemnites, which looked like squids, were marine molluscs of the cephalopod group. These molluscs were found in large numbers and in great variety in the Mesozoic seas, but disappeared at the Cretaceous-Tertiary boundary.

AMMONITE

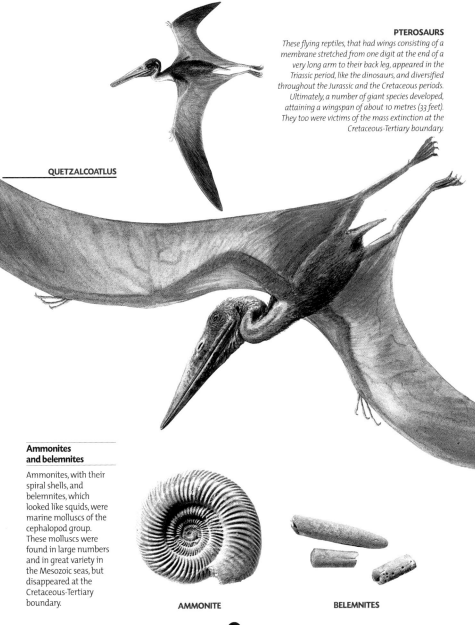

BELEMNITES

Controversial theories

Many of the theories put forward to explain the mass extinction do not stand up to scrutiny or are simply not worth considering. Some, however, have attracted attention and continue to be discussed by those who are unconvinced by the asteroid impact argument.

A PHASE OF INTENSE VOLCANIC ACTIVITY

It is known that around the time the dinosaurs disappeared, there were huge outpourings of basaltic lava from volcanoes in what is now western India. For 100,000 years or more, successive eruptions of lava covered a vast area of about 2.5 million square kilometres (1 million square miles) forming layer upon layer. Together with the lava, there would have been huge outpourings of gases, including carbon dioxide, and acid sulphur compounds.

It has been suggested that these caused changes, such as global warming, that led to the extinctions. It is certain that the local effects on the flora and fauna would have been huge, but scientists argue as to whether, for example, the amount of carbon dioxide gas would have been enough to cause change on a global scale. Interestingly, there are similar huge lava fields in Siberia dating back to about the time of the Permian-Triassic extinction.

THE THEORY OF DECCAN VOLCANIC ACTIVITY

THE THEORY OF MARINE REGRESSIONS

LOWERING OF SEA LEVELS

The theory is that a drastic drop in sea level at the end of the Cretaceous era would have limited the habitats on the continental shelf, causing extinctions of marine life. It would also have made continents larger, making their climate more 'continental' or extreme. This may have been bad for dinosaurs as well as other groups of animals on land.

In fact, sea levels have often shifted back and forth during the history of this planet, and some of these shifts happened during the time of the dinosaurs with no discernible effect on their ability to survive, or on sea creatures such as ammonites. In any case, right at the end of the Cretaceous period the sea levels were probably rising. Although sea level change must have affected local habitats quite drastically, it is difficult to imagine that it had a worldwide effect on sea and land.

GRADUAL CLIMATIC DETERIORATION

There is no real evidence in the rocks of a major cooling that would have made the Earth too cold for reptilian life. In any case we know that many reptiles, including types now confined to the tropics, such as crocodiles, survived the end of the Cretaceous period.

Some scientists have argued the opposite line: that the deterioration was due to an increase in temperature, that was enough to interfere with the reproductive processes of dinosaurs. In some living species of reptile, the temperature at which an egg is incubated affects the sex of the baby. Could the absence of one sex explain the dinosaurs' end? Even if it did, it does not account for all the other disappearances. Again, there is some evidence of warming just at the end of the Cretaceous period, but it appears too weak to have caused the observed extinctions.

The threat of meteorites, asteroids and comets

Proof of the collision of an enormous meteorite with the Earth 65 million years ago has been accumulating since 1980. The meteorite may have been a single asteroid, fragments resulting from asteroid collisions, or debris from a comet nucleus.

Showers of meteorites

These are not a rare event. It is estimated that the Earth receives more than 100,000 tons of cosmic material every day, but most of this burns up on entry into the Earth's atmosphere. Nevertheless, several hundred meteorites of considerable size reach the surface of the Earth each year. The impact of very large objects is, fortunately, much rarer.

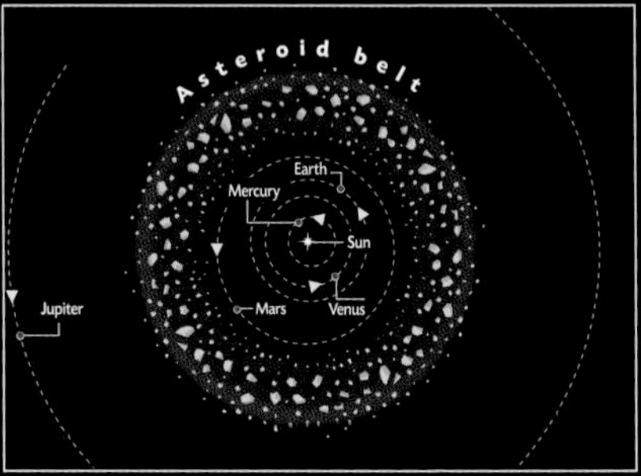

Meteorites

Several types of meteorite can be distinguished, depending on their composition. Some are referred to as stony, some as metallic, while others are a combination of the two.

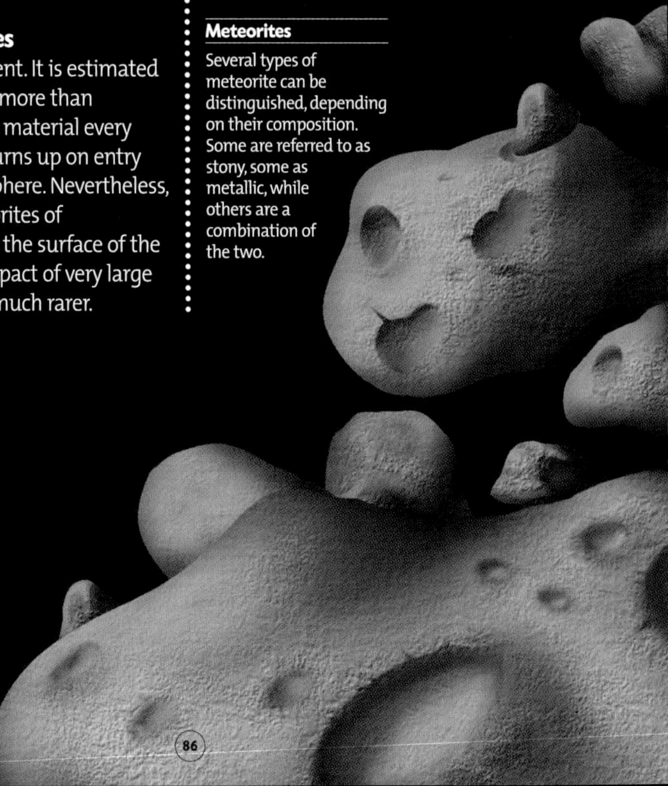

Asteroids

Many meteorites come from asteroids, which are celestial bodies whose size can vary from several metres wide to more than 1,000 kilometres (620 miles). In our solar system several thousand asteroids form a 'belt' situated between the orbits of Mars and Jupiter. This is a zone in which planets could not be created at the beginning of the formation of the solar system because of the gravitational pull of the giant planet Jupiter. As a result of collisions with each other, asteroid fragments may spin off and take orbits that cross with the Earth's orbit.

COMETS

Comets are celestial bodies possessing a nucleus of ice and rocks, which sometimes leads them to be called dirty snowballs. They have very flattened orbits around the Sun and when they get close to it they partially vaporise, producing huge tails of plasma spreading over massive distances. Comets can also enter the Earth's orbit, with the consequent risk of collision.

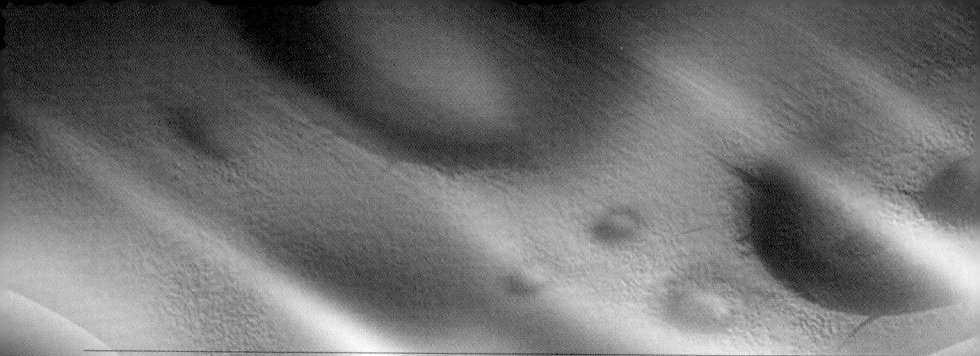

Extraterrestrial objects

Even if the atmosphere acts as an effective shield against smaller extraterrestrial objects, the larger ones reach the surface in the form of meteorites.

The dimensions of a crater

The size of the craters created by the largest meteorites is proportionate to the object's diameter. The meteorite generally leaves a crater approximately twenty times its width. These craters are formed by the enormous quantity of energy that is dissipated upon impact, by the meteorites striking the surface of the globe at extremely high speeds, and causing a violent explosion.

Visible signs

All the planets and satellites of the solar system are subject to meteorite impact, some showing visible traces of this. To take the most obvious example, the surface of the moon is riddled with impact craters. As the moon has no atmosphere and very little geological activity these craters have remained clearly visible for aeons. The same cannot be said of the Earth, where destruction or burial – either by tectonic activity, erosion or the build up of sediment – have contributed to the disappearance of impact traces. Nevertheless, some 150 meteorite impact craters have been located on the surface of our globe, of very varied sizes and ages, and their number continues to increase as research becomes ever more active in this field.

Detecting traces on Earth

The oldest craters are usually the hardest to spot. The great crater of Ries, in southern Germany, which was formed approximately 15 million years ago and which has a diameter of 25 kilometres (nearly 16 miles), was mainly filled in by lake sediment. Today it is an almost circular plain around the town of Nördingen, surrounded by a belt of low hills which formed the original edge of the crater. Older still is the crater of Rochechouart in Limousin, France, which dates back just over 200 million years; it is no longer visible, but was detected through geological research.

METEORITE CRATER

Some craters were formed (in geological terms) fairly recently, and those in desert regions still have clearly visible features. This is the case, for example, with the famous Meteorite Crater in Arizona, which is 1,200 metres (3,900 feet) wide and 190 metres (600 feet) deep. It was formed approximatley 50,000 years ago.

Meteorite craters

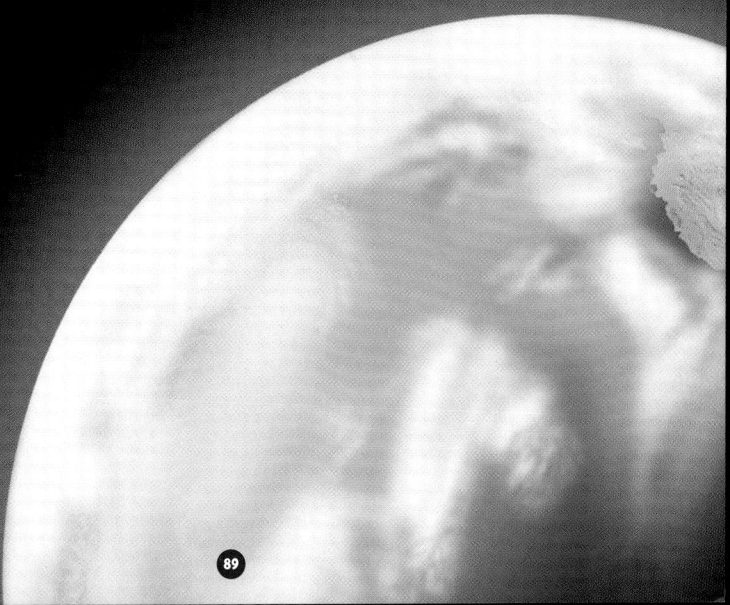

Signs of asteroid impact

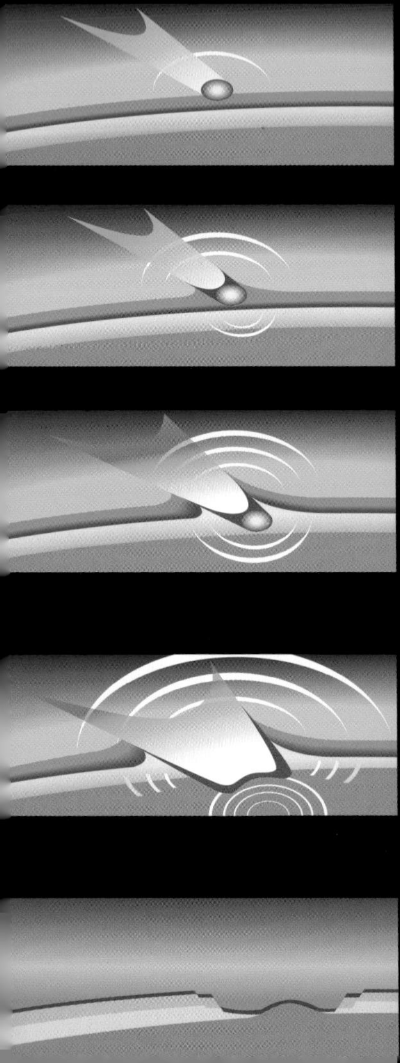

The first signs of the impact of an enormous meteorite, 65 million years ago, were discovered at the end of the 1970s. Since then, further confirmation has been found in many parts of the world. The telltale signs lie in a thin layer of clay, just 2–3 cm (about an inch) thick, between the rock beds laid down at the end of the Cretaceous period and the earliest rock beds of the Tertiary period. The clay contains elements which are rarely found on Earth.

Simulating the impact

In a laboratory of the NASA Space Agency, a researcher fired an aluminium projectile into a block of sand representing the Earth's crust. The idea was to simulate the kinds of damage that the planet might sustain from a falling meteorite.

Telltale deposits of iridium

A considerable quantity of iridium and other metals were found in the thin layer of clay deposited at the Cretaceous-Tertiary boundary. The iridium concentration in this thin layer is sometimes 100 times higher than in the rocks on either side. Although this metal is common in certain meteorites, it is rare in most of the Earth's rocks.

Droplets of molten rock

Other constituents of this layer of clay include small glassy spheres. They appear to be tektites – formed from droplets of molten rock projected into the atmosphere after a meteorite impact. These may travel considerable distances before falling back to earth.

Shocked quartz

Under the microscope, the clay layer shows quartz grains with very unusual abnormalities in their crystalline structure. Experiments have shown that in order to modify the crystal lattice of these minerals enormous pressure is required, equivalent to several million times atmospheric pressure. The only natural phenomena known to produce these sorts of pressures are meteorite impacts; even the most violent volcanic eruptions cannot generate what is known as shocked quartz.

Nickeliferous spinels

Very unusual magnetic nickel-bearing minerals known as nickel spinels are also to be found in this clay layer. This mineral is only formed in very specific conditions, namely when the surface of a meteorite is fused and oxidised on entering the atmosphere at high speed. These spinels at the Cretaceous-Tertiary boundary are therefore direct evidence of a meteorite.

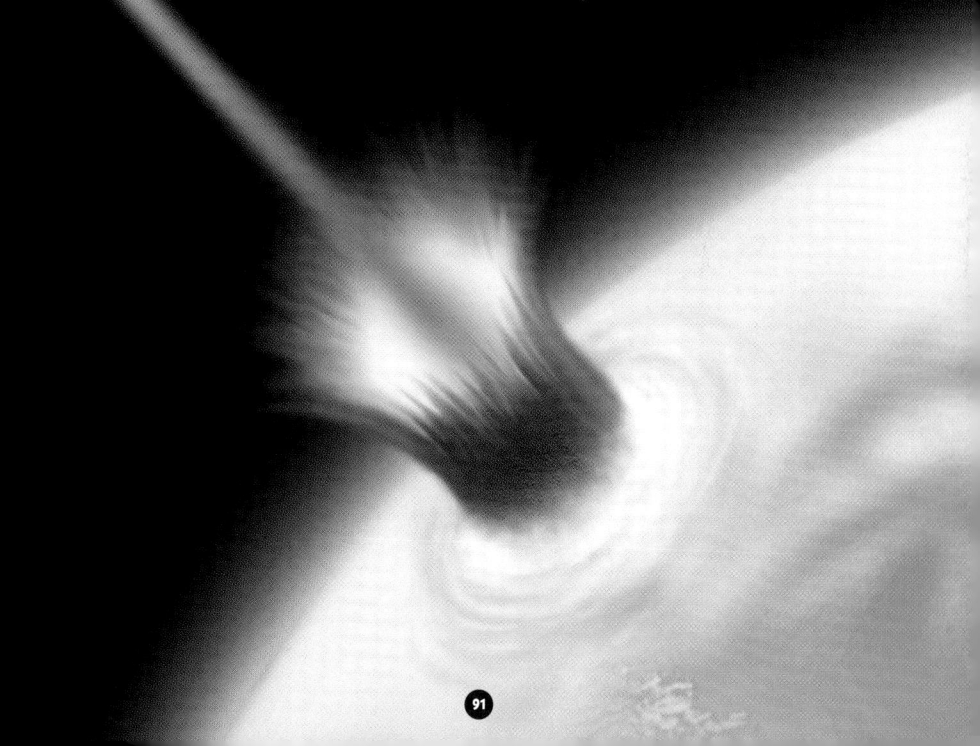

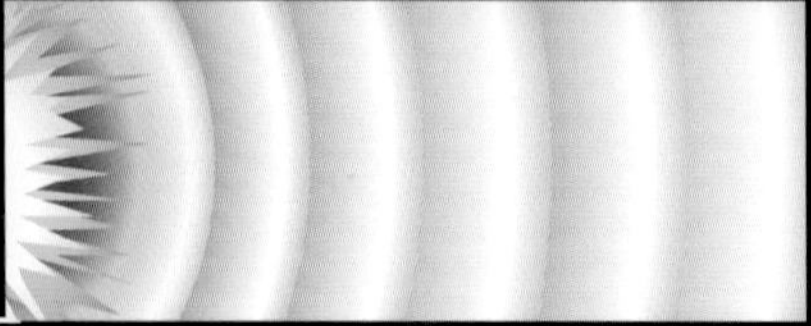

SHOCK WAVE

A titanic shock

Meteorites explode and crash into the Earth at vast speed, creating shock waves and forming craters.

WATER VAPORISES

Instant steam

Seas and lakes near the site of the impact are instantly vaporised.

ROCKS VAPORISE

A ball of fire

Vaporisation of meteorite and rock at the point of impact creates a gigantic ball of fire that reaches high into the atmosphere.

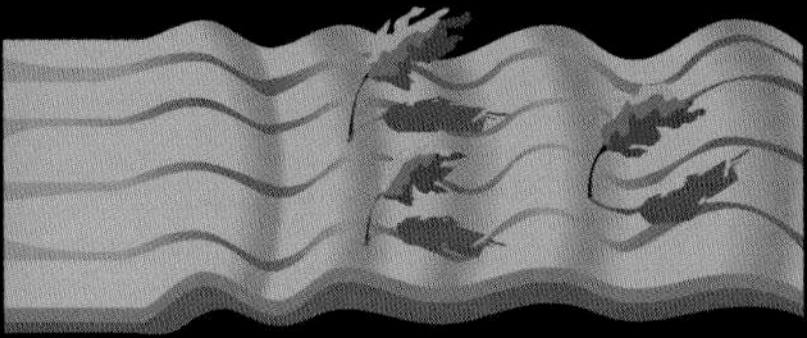

EARTHQUAKES

Earthquakes

Beyond the impact zone, shock waves ripple outward, producing huge earthquakes and landslides.

TSUNAMI (TIDAL WAVE)

Tsunami

Beyond the point of impact, the sea is hugely disturbed, causing great tidal waves, or tsunamis, on coasts thousands of kilometres away.

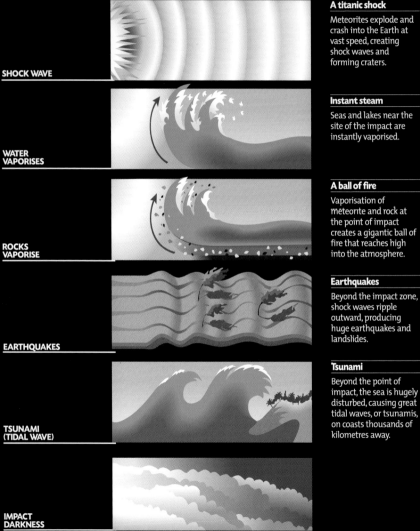

IMPACT DARKNESS

A chain of disasters

A deadly cloud

Probably the worst consequence of the meteorite's impact was the enormous amount of dust thrown up into the atmosphere. The dust was produced by the vaporisation both of the meteorite and the Earth's rocks at the point of impact. Shot into the stratosphere by the energy of the explosion, the dust spread over the whole globe. It created such a thick veil that it blocked out the sun's rays and plunged the surface of the Earth into darkness. This darkness must have lasted several months, until the dust finally fell slowly back to Earth. It remains visible as the layer of iridium-enriched clay that marks the Cretaceous-Tertiary boundary.

A deadly wave

The impact, located in the Gulf of Mexico, was followed by a colossal tsunami that swept the coasts of Central America and the southern part of North America. The devastation, which stretched for several thousand kilometres around, must have been total. Adding to the chaos, some researchers believe, was the sudden escape of methane gas from beneath the seabed, which had previously been trapped in layers of sediment. After impact, it escaped and ignited, adding to the fire storm.

Luckily, no human being has ever witnessed a disaster on the scale produced by the meteorite 65 million years ago. However, using what we know of geology and physics, it is possible to imagine the sequence of events.

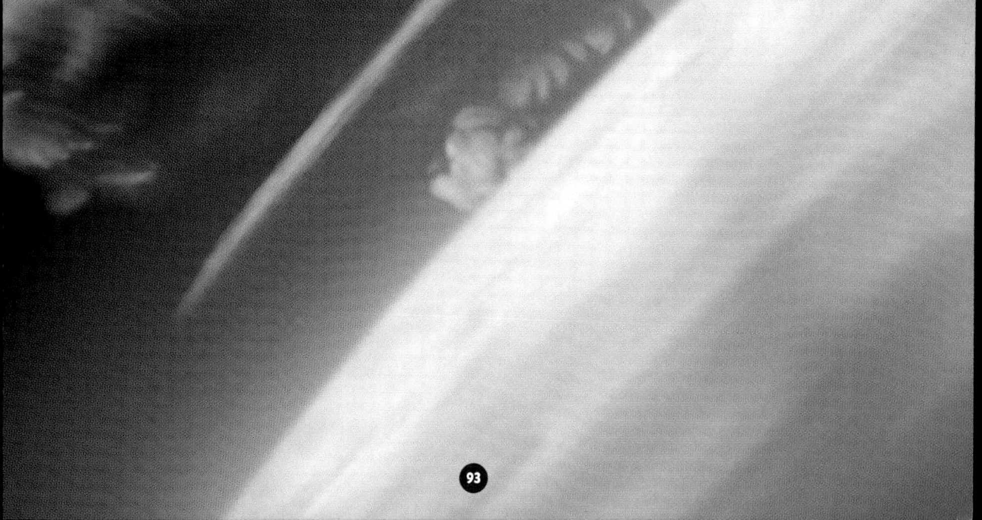

The effects of the darkness

One of the principal biological consequences of the dark, dust-induced conditions, was a break in the numerous food chains that initially depended on living plants.

Interrupting photosynthesis

Essential to plants, photosynthesis cannot take place without light. In the darkness that followed the impact, all plant life must have shrivelled up, causing severe and immediate consequences for those animal species that relied on plants for their food.

In the seas

Plant plankton, or phytoplankton, was the first to be affected by the lack of light, and its near-disappearance led to a break in a food chain that included animal plankton, then invertebrates such as ammonites and belemnites, various types of fish and, at the end of the chain, the great marine reptiles. It was the creatures that lived on the sea bed and fed on organic matter buried in the silt, like certain sorts of burrowing mollusc, that were better equipped to survive the disaster because they were not directly dependent on phytoplankton.

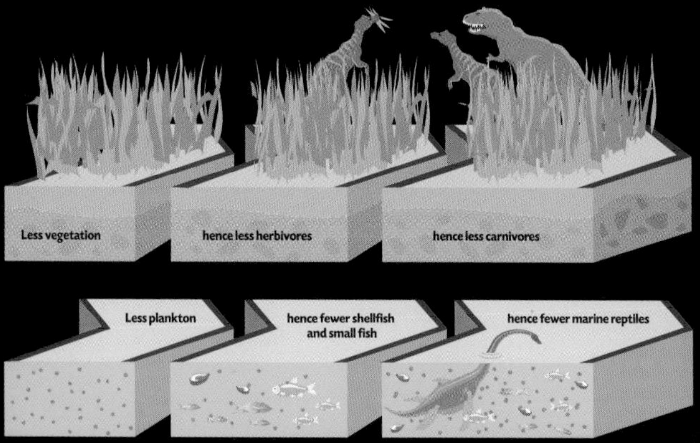
Less vegetation
hence less herbivores
hence less carnivores
Less plankton
hence fewer shellfish and small fish
hence fewer marine reptiles

BREAK IN THE FOOD CHAIN

1. Loss of plants, followed by the dying out of plant-eating dinosaurs, then of meat-eating dinosaurs.

2. Destruction of plankton, followed by fish dying out, then large marine reptiles.

On land

Plant life was devastated and the large herbivores (particularly herbivorous dinosaurs), which needed huge quantities of fresh plants to survive, disappeared because of the lack of food. The break in this link in the food chain led to the disappearance of carnivorous dinosaurs, who had been deprived of their prey.
In this scenario the extinction of the dinosaurs is the result of a temporary disappearance of food resources caused by the lack of sunlight. Those animals best placed to survive were part of other food chains that did not directly involve plant life.

Some plant species did survive

After several months, when the dust in the atmosphere had dissipated and light from the sun could reach the surface of the Earth again, most plants were able to start growing again, regenerating from the seeds, spores or rhizomes that had been able to survive the period of darkness. However, this was too late for the countless animal species that had died for lack of food.

The Chicxulub crater

Geophysical studies

Since 1991, studies of anomalies in the Earth's gravitational and magnetic fields have allowed scientists to trace an immense circular shape hidden below the surface of the Gulf of Mexico that extends on to the Yucatan peninsula. This is thought to be the remains of a crater. Near its centre is the little town of Chicxulub that gives its name (Mayan in origin) to the crater.

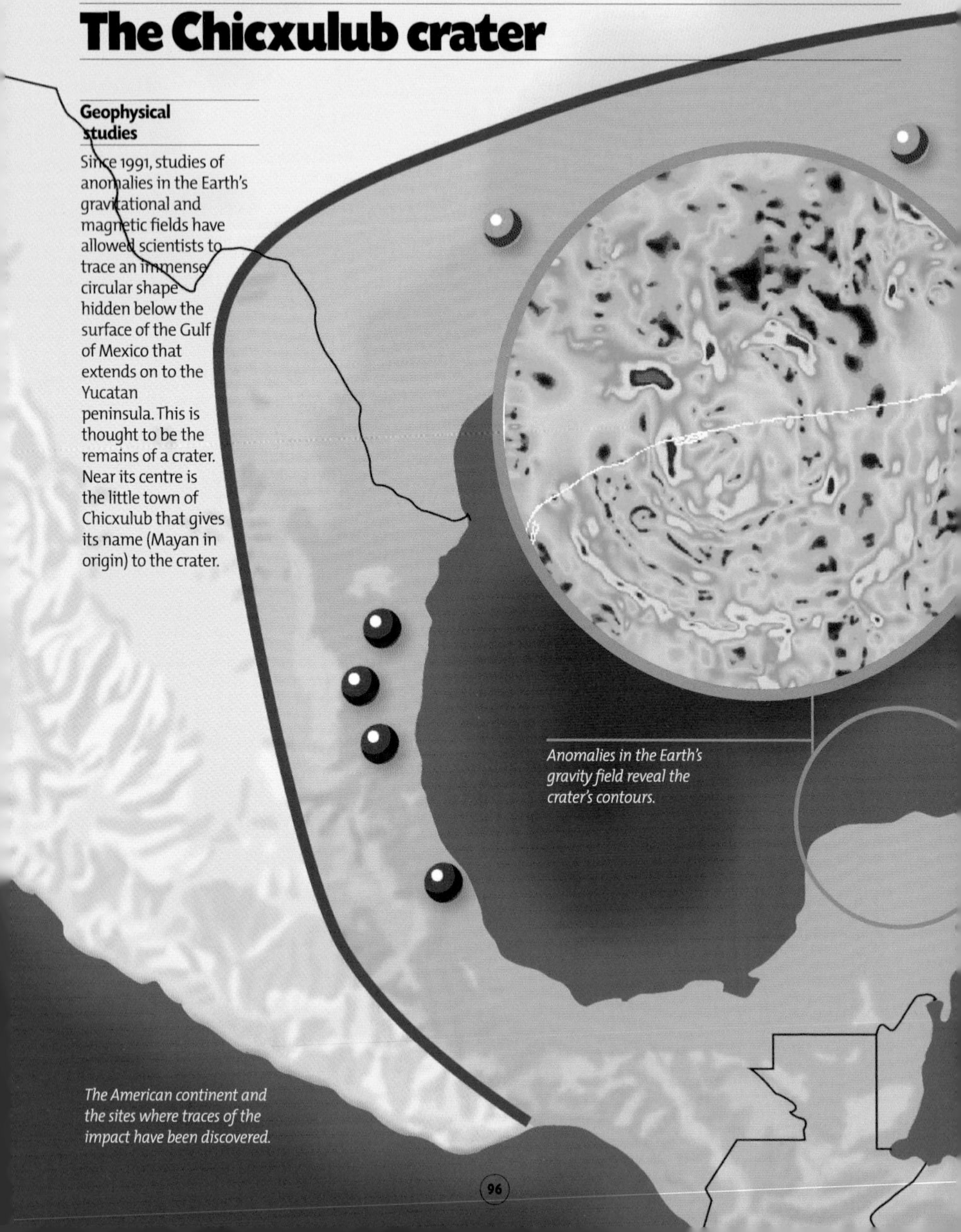

Anomalies in the Earth's gravity field reveal the crater's contours.

The American continent and the sites where traces of the impact have been discovered.

Traces of a tsunami

The rocks dating from the time of the Cretaceous-Tertiary boundary around the whole Gulf of Mexico area show traces of an enormous tsunami – tidal wave – in the form of deposits of coarse sand, carried high over the ancient shorelines of Central America and North America. At the same time, further north in New Jersey and in Florida, a layer of glass beads up to five centimetres (two inches) thick was deposited. Both phenomena point to a meteorite impact. The vast crater of Chicxulub, today eroded and filled in, is believed to be the point of the catastrophic impact that started many creatures on the road to extinction.

When an impact from a gigantic meteorite was suggested in 1980, following the discovery of unusual iridium deposits, the next problem was to find the crater. Palaeontologists were looking for something vast. Calculations suggested that a meteor ten kilometres (six miles) wide was needed to cause the destruction. If it hit the Earth it would result in a crater about 200 kilometres (125 miles) wide. For a dozen years or so the search was fruitless. At the beginning of the 1990s, however, a vast subterranean geological formation buried beneath the northern coast of the Yucatan peninsula in Mexico was hailed as the long-sought crater.

The first clues

A Mexican oil company carrying out a survey some years ago took measurements that might have led to the discovery of the crater – had that been the reason for the survey. Only later did the data help pinpoint the true nature of this particular geological structure.

The clues accumulate

The size of the crater was right and the oddities in the rocks of this period matched. Furthermore, the 'shocked' minerals found in the clay of the Cretaceous-Tertiary boundary from within North America, were found to have come from Chicxulub.

Life after the crisis

Once the dust from the impact had fallen back to Earth, life was not the same. It is estimated that 70 per cent of all species had disappeared, including dinosaurs, victims of breaks in the food chains and a decline in environmental conditions.

In water

Certain species, however, less affected by the disaster, survived relatively unscathed. These were, notably, animals that lived in fresh water and were part of a food chain that started with particles of organic matter suspended in water. These particles were consumed by small invertebrates such as worms and shellfish, themselves eaten by fish which, in turn, became prey for freshwater turtles and crocodiles.

On *terra firma*

Only small animals survived. They too formed part of food chains that were not dependent on living vegetation and were able to survive during the period of darkness. These were small vertebrates such as lizards and small mammals that fed on insects and worms, which in turn consumed the organic matter contained in the humus and the soil.

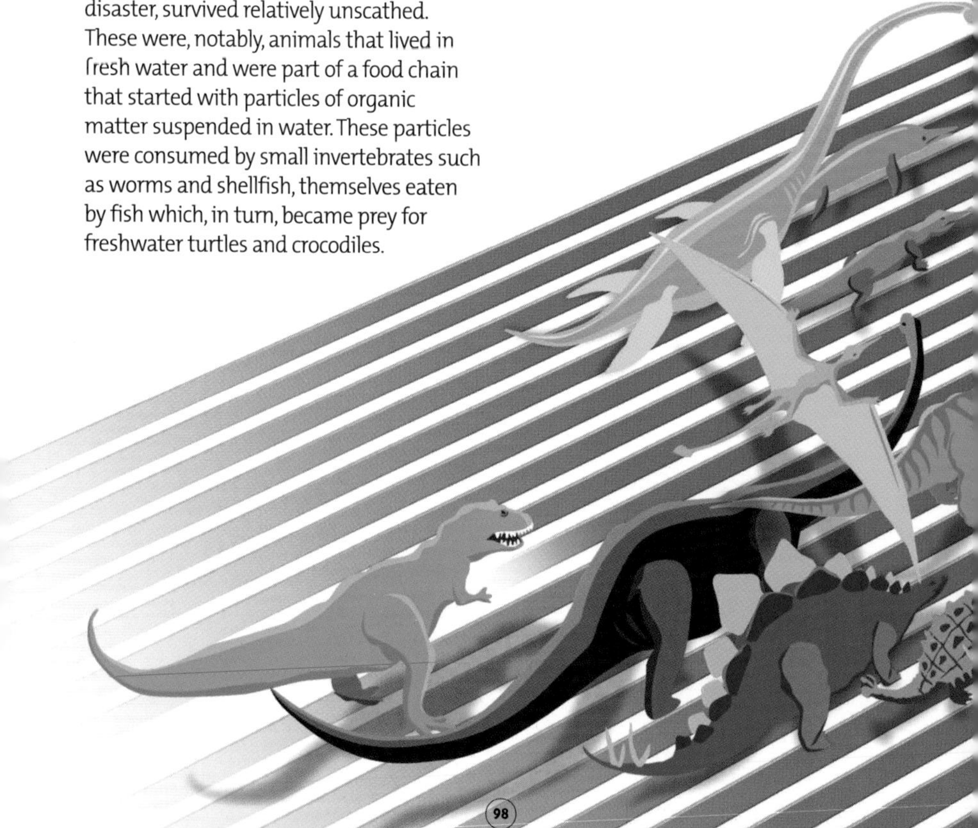

DIAGRAM SHOWING THE MASS EXTINCTION CAUSED BY THE CHICXULUB METEORITE

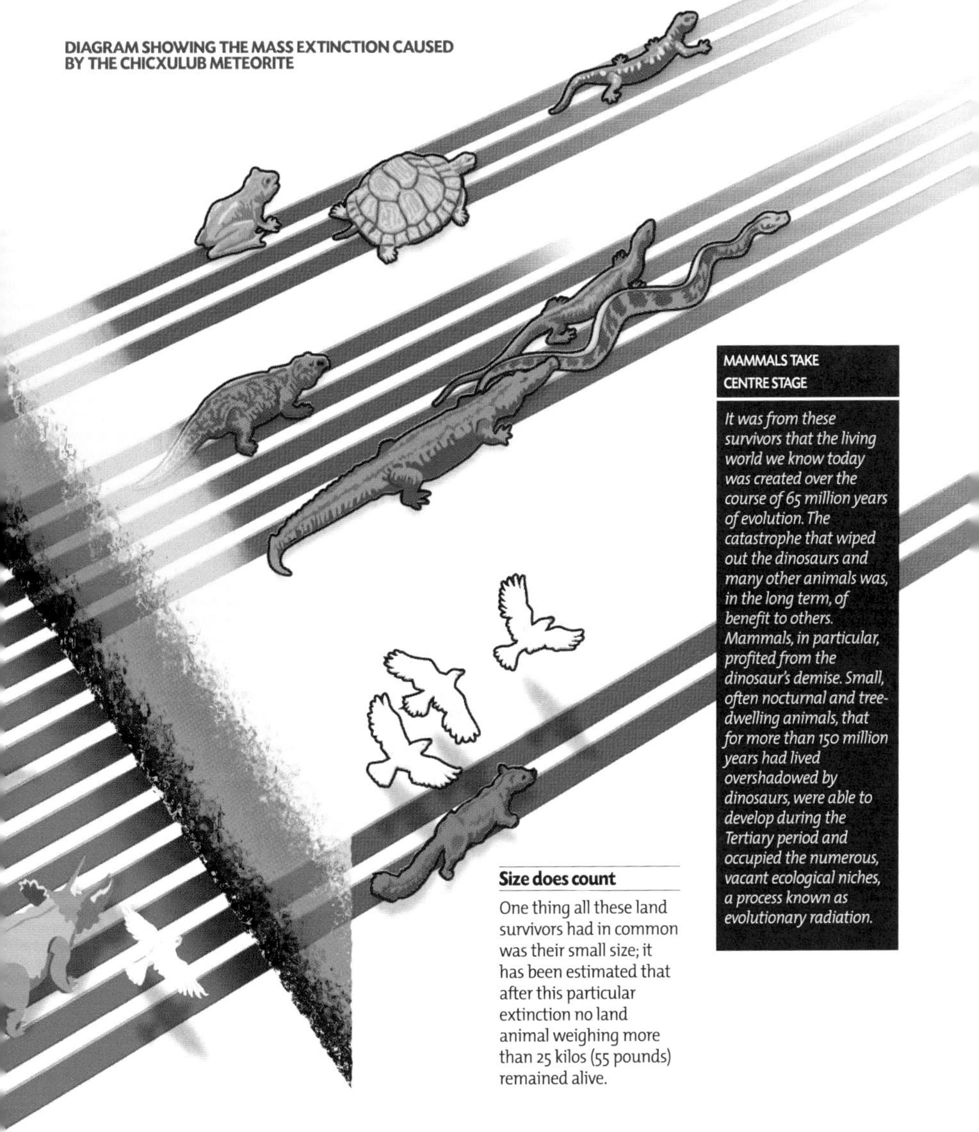

MAMMALS TAKE CENTRE STAGE

It was from these survivors that the living world we know today was created over the course of 65 million years of evolution. The catastrophe that wiped out the dinosaurs and many other animals was, in the long term, of benefit to others. Mammals, in particular, profited from the dinosaur's demise. Small, often nocturnal and tree-dwelling animals, that for more than 150 million years had lived overshadowed by dinosaurs, were able to develop during the Tertiary period and occupied the numerous, vacant ecological niches, a process known as evolutionary radiation.

Size does count

One thing all these land survivors had in common was their small size; it has been estimated that after this particular extinction no land animal weighing more than 25 kilos (55 pounds) remained alive.

The dinosaurs' descendants – from archaeopteryx to the pigeon

DROMAEOSAUR ('RUNNING DINOSAUR')

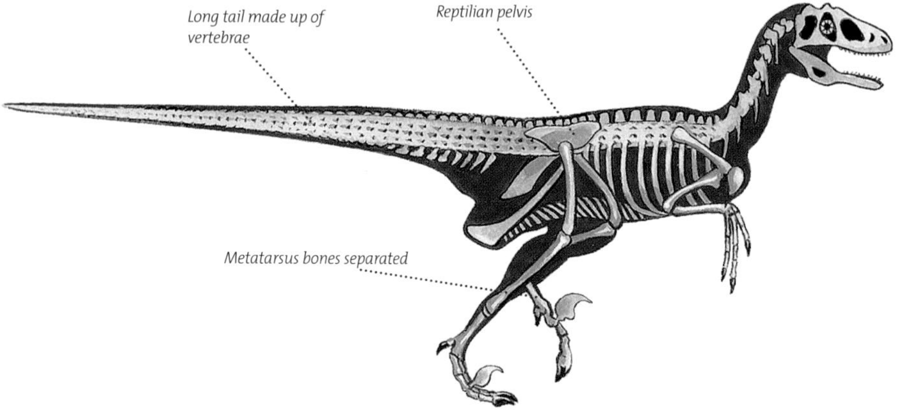

Did all the dinosaurs disappear 65 million years ago? It is sometimes tempting to seek the distant descendants of dinosaurs in some of the larger reptiles alive today, such as crocodiles or Komodo dragons. In fact, these animals, although distant relations of dinosaurs, are not their descendants.

Feathered dinosaurs

In order to find descendants of the dinosaurs in today's world, strange as it may seem, we need to turn to birds. In fact, the majority of today's palaeontologists think that birds are descended from certain small carnivorous dinosaurs. If the skeleton of the oldest known bird, Archaeopteryx, which lived about 140 million years ago, is compared to that of the dinosaurs, the resemblance is great. This has been confirmed by numerous recent finds of primitive birds that still had dinosaur features, and of dinosaurs that were close to birds. Some Chinese deposits from the beginning of the Cretaceous period, approximately 120 million years old, have even yielded the remains of animals that may have been dinosaurs with feathers.

ARCHAEOPTERYX

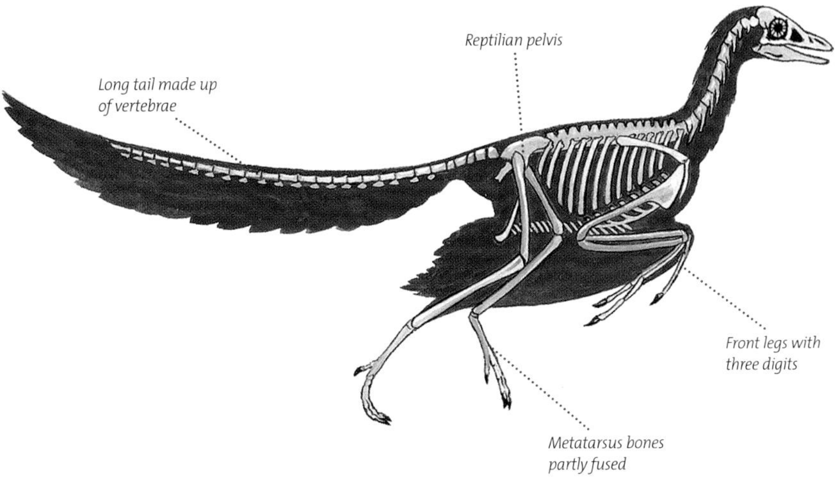

MODERN BIRD

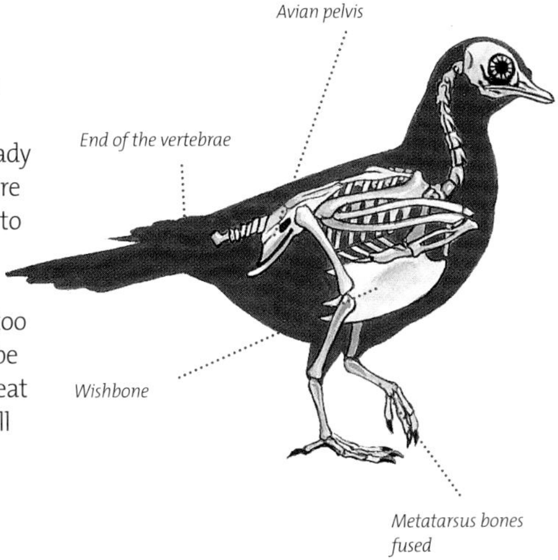

Birds already existed before the crisis

Fossils show us that at the time of the dinosaurs' disappearance, birds had already been in existence for a long time and were already very diversified. What happened to them when the disaster occurred? Experts have different opinions on this question, and the known fossils are still too few in number to allow the question to be resolved. However, it is possible that a great extinction took place among birds as well and that the group's evolution, when it started again at the beginning of the Tertiary period, was based only on a few surviving species.

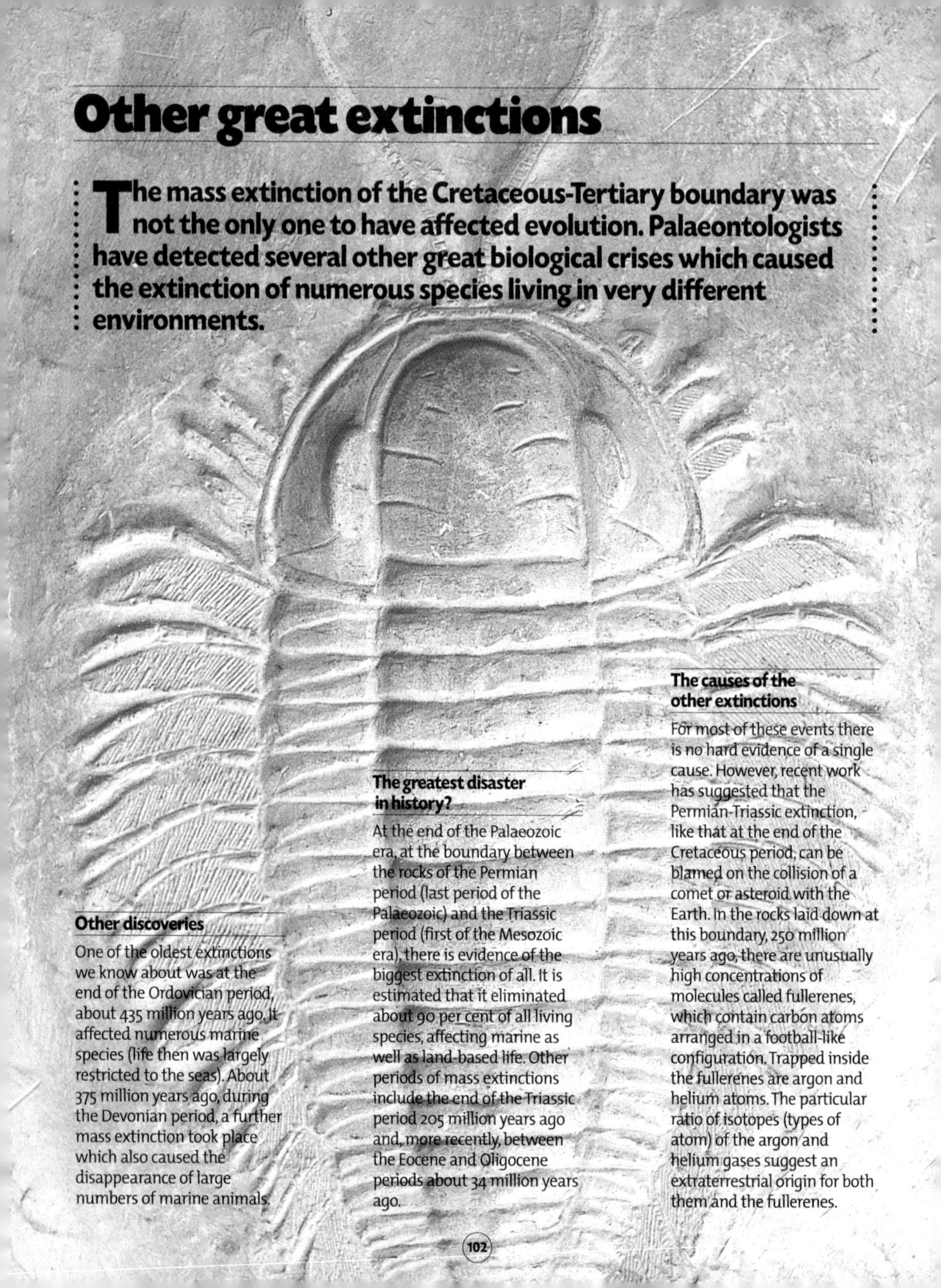

Other great extinctions

The mass extinction of the Cretaceous-Tertiary boundary was not the only one to have affected evolution. Palaeontologists have detected several other great biological crises which caused the extinction of numerous species living in very different environments.

Other discoveries

One of the oldest extinctions we know about was at the end of the Ordovician period, about 435 million years ago. It affected numerous marine species (life then was largely restricted to the seas). About 375 million years ago, during the Devonian period, a further mass extinction took place which also caused the disappearance of large numbers of marine animals.

The greatest disaster in history?

At the end of the Palaeozoic era, at the boundary between the rocks of the Permian period (last period of the Palaeozoic) and the Triassic period (first of the Mesozoic era), there is evidence of the biggest extinction of all. It is estimated that it eliminated about 90 per cent of all living species, affecting marine as well as land-based life. Other periods of mass extinctions include the end of the Triassic period 205 million years ago and, more recently, between the Eocene and Oligocene periods about 34 million years ago.

The causes of the other extinctions

For most of these events there is no hard evidence of a single cause. However, recent work has suggested that the Permian-Triassic extinction, like that at the end of the Cretaceous period, can be blamed on the collision of a comet or asteroid with the Earth. In the rocks laid down at this boundary, 250 million years ago, there are unusually high concentrations of molecules called fullerenes, which contain carbon atoms arranged in a football-like configuration. Trapped inside the fullerenes are argon and helium atoms. The particular ratio of isotopes (types of atom) of the argon and helium gases suggest an extraterrestrial origin for both them and the fullerenes.

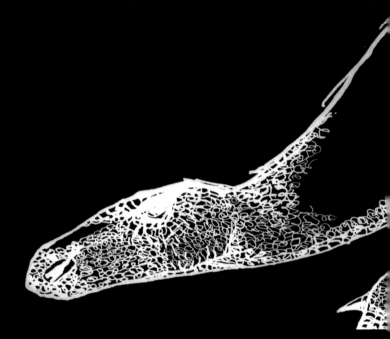

FIND OUT

THE DISCOVERIES OF PALAEONTOLOGISTS HAVE STIMULATED THE IMAGINATIONS OF WRITERS, PAINTERS AND FILM DIRECTORS, LEADING US TO WONDER WHETHER ANOTHER COLOSSAL ASTEROID COULD EVER CRASH INTO THE EARTH AGAIN. THERE ARE MUSEUMS, PARKS AND WEBSITES DEDICATED TO DINOSAURS TO HELP US DISCOVER WHAT LIFE WAS LIKE ON EARTH MILLIONS OF YEARS AGO.

Journey to the Centre of the Earth

Jules Verne

Axel, the hero of the novel, accompanies his uncle, geologist Otto Lidenbrock, on his journey into the depths of the Earth. He reaches the shore of a subterranean sea and sinks into a reverie that is inspired by the work of Cuvier.

'Thus it seems clear that this sea contains nothing but fossil species, in which fishes like reptiles are all the more completely developed the farther back they were created. Perhaps we may yet come across some of those saurians which scientists have constructed on the basis of a bit of bone or cartilage.

I took the telescope and examined the sea. It was deserted. No doubt we were still too near the shore.

I looked up in the air. Why should not some of those birds reconstructed by the immortal Cuvier be beating their wings in this dense atmosphere? The fish would provide them with sufficient food. I searched the space above me, but the air was as uninhabited as the shore.

Now, however, my imagination carried me away among the wonderful hypotheses of palaeontology, and I had a prehistoric dream. I fancied I could see floating on the water some huge chersites, antediluvian tortoises like floating islands. Along the dark shore there passed the great mammals of the early times, the leptotherium, found in the caves of Brazil, and the mercycotherium, found in the icy regions of Siberia. Farther on, the pachydermatous lophiodon, a gigantic tapir, was hiding behind the rocks, ready to dispute its prey with the anoplotherium, a strange animal which looked like an amalgam of rhinoceros, horse, hippopotamus and camel, as if the Creator, in too much of a hurry during the first hours of the world, had combined several animals in one. The giant mastodon waved its trunk and pounded the rocks on the shore with its tusks, while the megatherium, buttressed on its enormous legs , burrowed in the earth, rousing the echoes of the granite rocks with its roars. Higher up, the protopitheca, the first monkey to appear on earth, was climbing on the steep peaks. Higher still, the pterodactyl, with its winged claws, glided like a huge bat through the dense air. And finally, in the upper strata of the atmosphere, some enormous birds, more powerful than the cassowary and bigger than the ostrich, spread their vast wings and soared upwards to touch with their heads the ceiling of the granite vault.'

Journey to the Centre of the Earth, Jules Verne, 1864. Translated by Robert Baldick, Puffin, London, 1994, pp. 203–204 (translation first published by Penguin, London, in 1965).

The Lost World

Arthur Conan Doyle

A group of British explorers have reached an isolated plateau in South America and discover dinosaurs living there.

'An enormous three-toed track was imprinted in the soft mud before us. The creature, whatever it was, had crossed the swamp and had passed on into the forest. We all stopped to examine that monstrous spoor. If it were indeed a bird – and what animal could leave such a mark? – its foot was so much larger than an ostrich's that its height upon the same scale must be enormous. Lord John looked eagerly round him and slipped two cartridges into his elephant-gun.

'I'll stake my good name as a shikarree,' said he, 'that the track is a fresh one. The creature has not passed ten minutes. Look how the water is still oozing into that deeper print! By Jove! See, here is the mark of a little one!'

Sure enough, smaller tracks of the same general form were running parallel to the large ones.

'But what do you make of this?' cried Professor Summerlee, triumphantly, pointing to what looked like the huge print of a five-fingered human hand appearing among the three-toed marks.

'Wealden!' cried Challenger, in an ecstasy. 'I've seen them in the Wealden clay. It is a creature walking erect upon three-toed feet, and occasionally putting one of its five-fingered forepaws upon the ground. Not a bird, my dear Roxton – not a bird.'

'A beast?'

'No; a reptile – a dinosaur. Nothing else could have left such a track. They puzzled a worthy Sussex doctor some ninety years ago; but who in the world could have hoped – hoped – to have seen a sight like that?'
The Lost World, Arthur Conan Doyle, 1912.

The history of palaeontology

From the time of the very first discovery of strange fossils, it has taken nearly 300 years of patient research to establish a link between outer space and the disappearance of the dinosaurs.

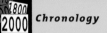

1705:The English scholar, Robert Hooke, claims that a large number of species found as fossils are now completely extinct.

1778: The Count of Buffon, in his *Époques de la Nature*, admits that certain species of animals have become extinct during the history of the Earth.

1794: German physicist Ernst Chladni declares that meteorites are of extraterrestrial origin.

1795: Georges Cuvier begins his work on fossil vertebrates and proves beyond doubt that many species are indeed extinct.

1803: After a meteor shower at L'Aigle (Orne, France), Jean-Baptiste Biot, in a report to the Académie des Sciences, concludes that objects from outer space really are landing on Earth.

1808: In a dissertation on the fossilised crocodiles of Normandy, Cuvier describes some dinosaur vertebrae which he believes to be those of a special sort of crocodile.

1812: Cuvier publishes the first edition of his *Recherches sur les Ossements Fossiles*, with Discours préliminaire as a preamble in which he expounds his ideas on 'global revolutions' and the extinctions they caused.

1824: William Buckland, a palaeontologist from Oxford, describes Megalosaurus, the first dinosaur to receive a scientific name.

1825: Gideon Mantell, an English surgeon, writes about the Iguanodon, a plant-eating dinosaur.

1830: The Scottish geologist, Charles Lyell, publishes the first volume of his *Principles of Geology*, in which he disagrees with catastrophe theories.

1842:The British anatomist and palaeontologist, Richard Owen, suggests the term 'Dinosauria' (terrible lizards) to describe a group of large reptile fossils from the Mesozoic era.

1859: Charles Darwin publishes *On the Origin of Species by Means of Natural Selection*, in which he sets out his views on the evolution of species and takes issue with the theory of catastrophism.

1905: The American engineer, D.M. Barringer, concludes that the large crater in Arizona is of meteoric origin.

1908: The Tunguska event. The explosion of a meteor over Siberia causes widespread devastation, the first demonstration in modern times of the catastrophic damage that could be caused by an extraterrestrial object.

1921: Alfred Wegener, originator of the theory of continental drift, concludes that the craters of the moon were formed by meteorite strikes.

1956: MW de Laubenfels suggests that dinosaurs may have been the victims of a meteorite impact.

1980: As a consequence of the discovery of unusually high levels of iridium at the Cretaceous-Tertiary boundary, Walter Alvarez, Frank Asaro and Helen Michel come up with the theory that the impact of an enormous meteorite caused the extinction of the dinosaurs at the same time.

1991: Alan Hildebrand and his collaborators announce the discovery of the crater of Chicxulub in Mexico, considered to be the proof of the impact that occurred at the Cretaceous-Tertiary boundary.

The great dinosaur detectives

Enthusiastic amateurs, adventurers and scientists have all helped in unlocking the mystery of the dinosaurs.

Georges Cuvier (1769-1832)

A professor at the Natural History Museum in Paris, Cuvier established the scientific basis of vertebrate palaeontology by applying comparative anatomy to fossilised bones. From this, he was able to prove that numerous animal species had become extinct in the course of time. He believed that the species that had become extinct, had been wiped out by 'global revolutions', and his catastrophist theories, Cuvier's work heralded present-day research on mass extinctions.

Gideon Mantell (1790-1852)

An English physician, Mantell was one of the pioneers of dinosaur science. He discovered and described many dinosaur remains from the Cretaceous period found in south-east England (including Iguanodon, Hylaeosaurus and Pelorosaurus). The story goes that Mrs Mantell actually found the first Iguanodon fossils, a few teeth lying in a pile of stones to be used for road repairs, while waiting outside a house for her husband, who was attending to a patient inside. Mantell searched museums and books to find out what the teeth came from, and received plenty of misleading advice, before seeing some teeth from an iguana. He then concluded that the teeth probably came from a gigantic reptile. Mantell was among the first to realise that the Mesozoic was an 'age of reptiles', dominated in particular by dinosaurs.

Richard Owen (1804-1892)

In 1842 the British anatomist and palaeontologist Richard Owen put forward the name 'Dinosauria' (terrible lizards) to embrace several large reptile fossils whose remains had been found in England. He was famous for his ability to predict the size, shape and habits of an animal from just a fragment of the skeleton. He had some spectacular successes with this method, although his ideas were limited by the material available. After the Great Exhibition of 1851 in London, the great glasshouse known as the 'Crystal Palace' was moved to a park in the area of London now named after it. Owen was asked to advise on life-size models of giant reptiles to be placed in the park. They are still there, but some are a long way from modern ideas of what the animals looked like. However, Owen was one of the first to note the fact that dinosaurs' straight limbs separated them from present-day reptiles.

Walter Alvarez

It was while studying the sediments deposited at the Cretaceous-Tertiary boundary in Italy, that this American geologist discovered the iridium-enriched level that became the first sign of the asteroid impact at the end of the Cretaceous period. In 1980, with his father, physicist Luis Alvarez, and geochemists Frank Asaro and Helen Michel, he published a classic article in the journal *Science*. It set out the theory of an impact at the Cretaceous-Tertiary boundary, marking the starting point of the new catastrophist geology.

Georges Cuvier

Palaeontology – at the crossroads of the sciences

Palaeontology is the study of fossils, in other words, the remains of living creatures, or traces of their activity found in the rocks of the Earth's crust. It is a discipline that is placed mid-way between life sciences and earth sciences. The palaeontologist therefore has to be both a biologist and a geologist.

Training for the job

In Britain, most palaeontologists will have done a first degree in either geology or a biological science. In addition, many will have taken a further three years to achieve a doctorate in some aspect of palaeontology. Some work in firms in the oil or mining sectors, but museums and universities employ most of those that study large fossils such as dinosaurs. The number of such jobs is relatively small. A palaeontologist needs to master a broad diversity of approaches and techniques, because of the variety of objects that need to be studied; one day they might be dealing with heavy-boned dinosaurs, the next with microscopic grains of pollen. Some palaeontologists prefer carrying out research in the field, others are to be found mostly in their laboratories employing a variety of modern equipment to study fossils. Some palaeontologists are more interested in theoretical aspects of the science – although theorists would have nothing to speculate about if others had not collected fossils in the first place.

Working in the field

Research can lead palaeontologists to a variety of places, from cliffs on the south coast of Devon to deserts in southern Tunisia, vineyards in Languedoc or the jungles of Thailand. There is no guaranteed way of finding fossils and luck plays a large part in their discovery. Sometimes they are the result of a chance find by someone taking a walk, or they are accidentally unearthed by workmen, or collected by a geologist or a fossil hunter. Investigating the initial discovery is often the first job of the palaeontologist. It involves making a systematic search, scouring the whole area for signs of the presence of fossils; fragments of bone which only a practised eye can distinguish may be indications of the existence of important fossil sites, likely to yield whole skeletons. This prospecting work may become exhausting and boring when it entails walking for hours in the sun or the rain without any significant results. However, it can also lead to a great sense of achievement when it meets with success.

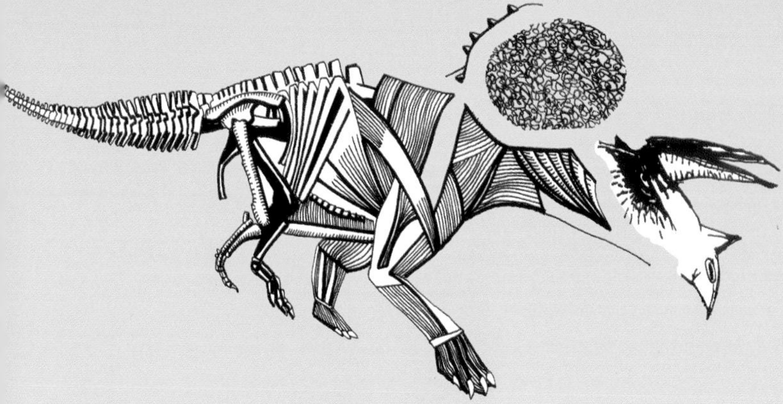

Noting all the details on site

Locating a fossil site is only the beginning of a palaeontologist's work. Even if some of the fossils can be removed without too much difficulty, it is essential, in order to obtain all the necessary scientific information, to note every detail of their location and the geology of their surroundings. However, to be able to extract a number of fossils successfully, special techniques have to be employed in order to ensure that the specimens reach the laboratory in the best possible condition. This is particularly true of fossilised bones, which are generally extremely crumbly and fragile.

Getting fossils to talk

Up to this point the work of the palaeontologist, both in the field and in the laboratory, is largely technical. The most challenging aspect of the work comes later, once the cleaned specimen is in the hands of the scientist, who now tries to make the fossil reveal its secrets. The key word here is comparison: to identify a fossil, it has first of all to be compared to the various kinds of fossil that are already known, because they have already been described in the huge quantity of palaeontological literature that has accumulated over the last two centuries. Although the general public is largely unaware of this, book-based research is one of the crucial aspects of a palaeontologist's work. However, referring to published literature and existing illustrations is not always enough, and often scientists have to turn to the vast palaeontology collections in museums all over the world in order to make their comparisons. The need to identify some dinosaur remains found in Thailand, for example, led the author of this book to museums in New York, Berlin, Warsaw, Beijing and Ulan Bator. However, the identification of a specimen, establishing whether it can be related to a species that is already known, or whether it has to be given a new name, is only the beginning. Palaeontology also involves understanding where creatures stand on the evolutionary ladder, trying to find their possible ancestors and descendants, reconstructing their way of life and the environment in which they evolved, relocating them in fact, in the framework of the history of our planet and its changing circumstances. Cuvier spoke of 'resuscitating' fossils; this is what palaeontologists are still attempting to do today, at the end of a long process that starts in the dust of an archaeological dig and ends in a museum.

The return of the asteroids – could it happen again?

Shall we too, one day, share the same grim fate as the dinosaurs? An enormous comet or asteroid colliding with the Earth would effectively release as much energy as millions of atomic bombs, and large numbers of species would be wiped out once and for all, exactly as happened at the time of the dinosaurs.

Tunguska, Siberia

On 30 June 1908, at 7.17 am, an extraordinary event devastated a large part of the region of Tunguska in Siberia which, fortunately, was practically uninhabited. A gigantic explosion flattened and burnt to a crisp all the trees up to 30 kilometres (18 ½ miles) away. At a distance of 50 kilometres (31 miles) the blast destroyed cabins, knocking their inhabitants to the ground. According to reports at the time, some people were injured and two may have died. Those witnessing it, mostly Siberian nomads, said they saw a ball of fire in the sky, accompanied by a deafening noise. The sky was lit up by the explosion to such an extent that the glare from it was visible in England. The cause of this phenomenon was the subject of endless discussion, even more so since the first Russian scientific expedition to the region did not take place until 1924, and found no trace of a crater. It is thought today that the cause was the explosion of a meteorite of the chondrite group (ie a granular meteorite) in the lower atmosphere, with a force of about 1,000 times the atomic bomb dropped on Hiroshima. If the meteorite had arrived at the same latitude four hours and fifty-two minutes later, the explosion would have destroyed St Petersburg and claimed hundreds of thousands of victims.

A rare disaster

The example of the Tunguska event shows that a large meteorite strike is not just something that occurred in the distant past. It is known that quite large asteroids cross the orbit of the Earth every so often and that the risk of a collision cannot be ruled out. Programmes for astronomical research and the detection of such objects were launched several years ago. These have made it possible to identify more than a hundred and fifty asteroids more than 50 metres (164 feet) in diameter which have entered the Earth's orbit. Periodically the press picks up on announcements made by astronomers of long-term collision risks (although the announcements are usually quickly forgotten). Plans to destroy or divert these objects before a collision can take place have also been put forward.

But can serious estimates be made of the risks run by human civilisation, or of life on our planet, from the impacts of meteorites? It has been estimated that the Earth could have been hit on average every 100 million years by a meteorite of about ten kilometres (six and a quarter miles) in diameter, which would cause a disaster comparable to the catastrophe of the Cretaceous-Tertiary boundary. The frequency of meteorite impacts of around one-and-a-half kilometres (one mile) in diameter would, of course, be greater, in the order of every 500,000 years. At any rate, these are extremely rare events on the human scale and there is no point in trying to take out insurance against the risk of being hit by a meteorite!

Further extinction theories

The argument developed in this book is supported by a growing number of discoveries. However, dozens of others exist, which range from the totally improbable to the more or less convincing. Here's a selection ...

The swamps the dinosaurs were thought to live in dried up.

Epidemics exterminated the dinosaurs.

At the end of the Cretaceous period, small mammals began eating dinosaur eggs which eventually brought about their downfall.

The climate became too cold.

The climate became too hot.

dinosaurs...

...were the victims of competition with mammals.

... were killed by newly-evolved poisonous plants.

...were the victims of a cataract epidemic which made them go blind.

... were exterminated by the radiation released by a nearby solar supernova.

... could not adapt to a new plant world dominated by flowering plants.

... couldn't get a place on Noah's Ark.

...were exterminated by extraterrestrials.

... died of starvation when the plants they fed on were devoured by caterpillars.

...died out because of hormonal problems leading to gigantism, the development of horns, scales and other unnecessary structures.

... were the victims of hormonal problems leading them to lay abnormal eggs (with shells too thin or too thick) which did not allow the embryos to develop.

...were the victims of racial senescence (a species simply growing old).

... were especially stupid, which caused them to disappear.

... were unable to adapt and were doomed to extinction.

... died out through overpopulation.

... were the victims of parasites.

The Fossil Elephant

Mary Howitt

The earth is old! Six thousand years,
Are gone since I had birth;
In the forests of the olden time,
And the solitudes of earth.

We were a race of mighty things;
The world was all our own.
I dwell with the Mammoth large and strong,
And the giant Mastodon.

No ship went over the waters then,
No ship with oar or sail;
But the wastes of the sea were habited
By the Dragon and the Whale.

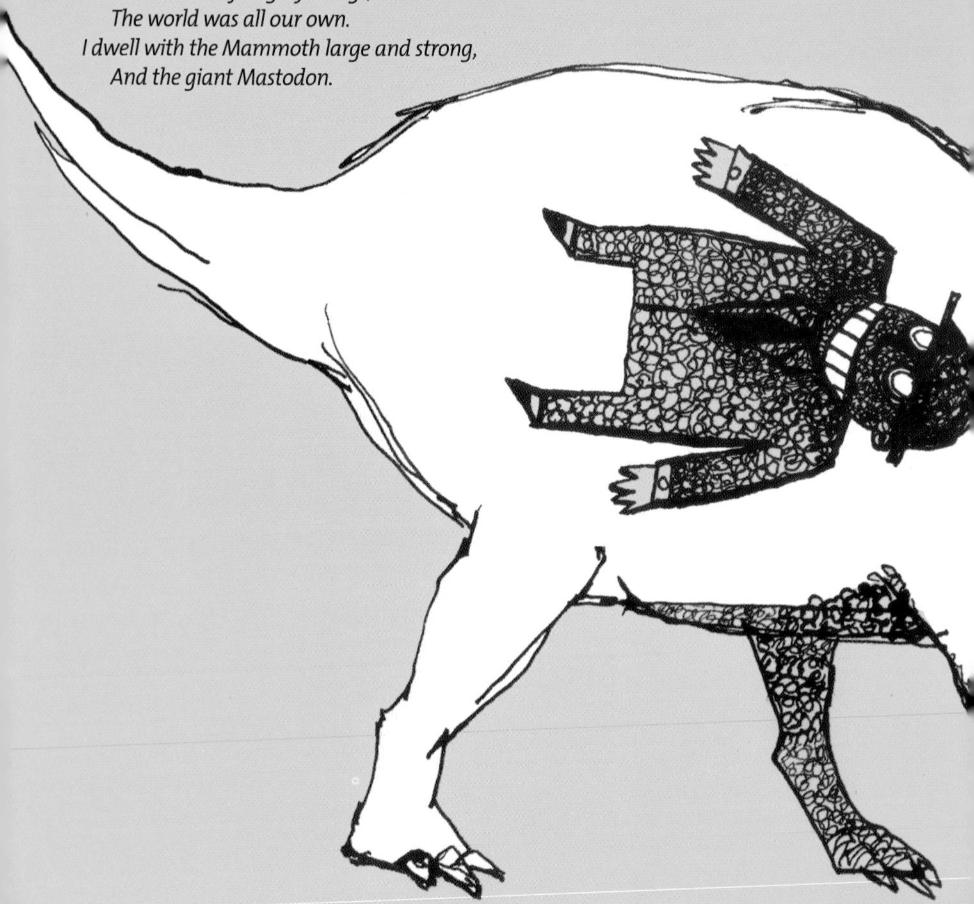

And the Hydra down in the ocean caves
Abode, a creature grim;
And the scaled Serpents huge and strong
Coiled up in the waters dim.

The wastes of the world were all our own;
A proud and imperial lot!
Man had not then dominion given,
Or else we knew it not.

There was no city on the plain;
No fortress on the hill;
No mighty men of strength, who came
With armies up, to kill.

There was no iron then – no brass –
No silver and no gold;
The wealth of the world was in its woods,
And its granite mountains old.

And we were the kings of all the world
We knew its breadth and length;
We dwelt in the glory of solitude,
And the majesty of strength.

But suddenly came an awful change!
Wherefore, ask not of me;
That it was, my desolate being shews, –
Let that suffice for thee.

The Mammoth huge and the Mastodon
Were buried beneath the earth;
And the Hydra and the Serpents strong,
In the caves where they had birth!

There is now no place of silence deep,
Whether on land or sea;
And the Dragons lie in the mountain-rock,
As if for eternity!

And in the far realms of thawless ice,
Beyond each island shore,
My brethren lie in the darkness stern
To awake to life no more!

And not till the last conflicting crash
When the world consumes in fire,
Will their frozen sepulchres be loosed,
And their dreadful doom expire!

From *Sketches of Natural History*

Dinosaurs of the silver screen

Dinosaurs made their appearance on cinema screens shortly after the Lumière Brothers invented cinematography in 1895. Since then, they have had a prolific career. Different techniques have been used to show dinosaurs on the screen: animated cartoons, stop-frame animation models, and even the use of live reptiles 'made up' with artificial horns and crests, until the use of computer-generated images superseded all the more dated special effects.

GERTIE THE DINOSAUR

Winsor McCay, 1912: as well as being one of the first cartoons, this was one of the first films to include a scene with a dinosaur. The film, by the American animator Winsor McCay, features a tame sauropod as its hero.

THE LOST WORLD

Harry Hoyt, 1925: openly taking its inspiration from Arthur Conan Doyle's novel (1912), in which explorers discover dinosaurs living in South America, this film shows various dinosaurs animated by Willis O'Brien, including a sauropod sowing panic in the streets of London, following a broadly similar storyline.

KING KONG

Ernest Schoedsack, 1933: on the island where the giant gorilla reigns, the heroes of the film also discover several dinosaurs, portrayed according to the popular conceptions of the time and created in stop-frame animation by Willis O'Brien, the great master of this technique. The film also showed some spectacular fights between different giant reptiles.

FANTASIA

Walt Disney, 1940: an amazing sequence from this musical cartoon shows the world of the dinosaurs set to the score of Igor Stravinsky's Rite of Spring. The end of the sequence shows the dinosaurs dying of thirst in a world dried out by an increasingly hot climate, adopting a theory that was popular at the time.

GODZILLA

Inoshiro Honda, 1954: a gigantic dinosaur-like monster ravages Tokyo. The first of a long series of Japanese films showing these monsters, this is a masterpiece of low-budget special effects and cinematic kitsch.

JOURNEY TO THE CENTRE OF THE EARTH

Henry Levin, 1959: in this film, based on the novel by Jules Verne (1864), the prehistoric reptiles encountered by the explorers of the huge subterranean world were actually live lizards that were enlarged and transformed by the addition of artificial crests and spikes!

ONE MILLION YEARS B.C.

Don Chaffey, 1967: a film based on the inaccurate premise that dinosaurs and prehistoric man were alive at the same time; appreciated at the time for the sight of Raquel Welch in a fur bikini and the quality of the stop-frame animation by Ray Harryhausen, a worthy successor to Willis O'Brien.

THE VALLEY OF GWANGI

James O'Connolly, 1969: at the turn of the century a group of cowboys discover a valley in Mexico populated by dinosaurs. They capture an Allosaurus and exhibit it in a circus, from which it soon escapes, finally perishing in a fire in a cathedral. The storyline is not very realistic, but the animation by Ray Harryhausen certainly is.

JURASSIC PARK

Steven Spielberg, 1993: taken from an novel by Michael Crichton, this film brings dinosaurs back to life twice over: once, through the genetic manipulation carried out by the characters in the film, and secondly through the excellent computer-generated images, used here for the first time in such a successful way to show dinosaurs on the screen.

THE LOST WORLD

Steven Spielberg, 1997: a film taken, unfortunately from the novel of the same title by Michael Crichton and not the one by Arthur Conan Doyle. The quality of the computer-generated images do not compensate for the lack of storyline.

T.REX: BACK TO THE CRETACEOUS

Brett Leonard, 1998: a semi-documentary film for the large screen, using Imax techniques, featuring computer-generated images to show various dinosaurs, including the famous Tyrannosaurus Rex. This film is one of the first to explain the disappearance of dinosaurs due to the earth being hit by a meteorite.

Websites

There are a large number of websites related to dinosaurs, including quite a few unofficial ones created by palaeontologists or other enthusiasts. Many natural history museums with dinosaur collections also have websites. The following selection is a starting point, allowing you to browse for more information on dinosaurs, meteorite impacts and extinctions.

DINOSAUR MUSEUM OF ESPÉRAZA
www.dinosauria.org/index_us.htm
This site shows the activities of this museum, which is dedicated to dinosaurs, and gives links to other sites on the subject.

DINOBASE
www.palaeo.gly.bris.ac.uk/dinobase/dinomenu.html
Site of the University of Bristol, with a very detailed catalogue of dinosaurs, as well as pages on extinction theories.

PAPER DINOSAURS
www.lhl.lib.mo.us/pubserv/hos/dino/welcome.htm
This site displays images of the evolution of dinosaur reconstructions since the beginning of the 19th century, drawn from rare books and catalogues.

THE MUSEUM OF PALEONTOLOGY, UNIVERSITY OF CALIFORNIA AT BERKELEY
www.ucmp.berkeley.edu
An excellent dinosaur resource centre.

DISCOVERING DINOSAURS
www.dinosaur.eb.com
Shows the history of the development of our knowledge of dinosaurs.

WALKING WITH DINOSAURS
www.bbc.co.uk/dinosaurs/dig_deeper/index.shtml
Fact files, games and dinosaur news updates.

TALKING ABOUT DINOSAURS
www.newscientist.com/nsplus/insight/rexfiles
Articles from New Scientist magazine about the latest thinking on the subject of dinosaurs and related topics.

METEORITES AND IMPACT CRATERS
www.nearctica.com/geology/meteor.htm
Supplies a list of sites on this subject.

METEORS, METEORITES AND IMPACTS
www.sedsorg/nineplanets/nineplanets/meteorites/html
Meteorites and their impacts, with links to other meteor sites.

Further reading

W. Alvarez, *T. Rex and the Crater of Doom*, Princeton University Press, 1997.

M.J. Benton, ed. and others, *The Age of the Dinosaurs in Russia and Mongolia*, CUP, 2001.

D. Cadbury, *The Dinosaur Hunters*, Fourth Estate, 2000

V. Courtillot, C. Allege, *Evolutionary Catastrophes*, CUP, 1999.

C. Frankel, *The End of the Dinosaurs*, CUP, 1999.

T. Gardom & A. Milner, *The Natural History Museum Book of Dinosaurs*, Carlton Books, 2000.

T. Haines, *Walking with Dinosaurs*, BBC Consumer Publishing, 1999.

A. Hallam & P. Wignall, *Mass Extinctions and their Aftermath*, OUP, 1997.

D. Lambert, *The Ultimate Dinosaur Book*, Dorling Kindersley, 1993.

D. Norman & P. Welnhoffer, *The Illustrated Encyclopedia of Dinosaurs and Pterosaurs*, Salamander Books, 2000.

D. Palmer, *Atlas of the Prehistoric World*, Marshall Publishing, 2000.

D. Palmer and others, *The Simon & Schuster Encyclopedia of Dinosaurs and Prehistoric Creatures: A Who's Who of Prehistoric Life*, Simon & Schuster Books, 1999.

J. L. Powell, *Night Comes to the Cretaceous: Comets, Craters, Controversy and the Last Days of the Dinosaurs*, Harvest Books, 1999.

M. J. S. Rudwick, trans., *Georges Cuvier, Fossil Bones, and Geological Catastrophes*, University of Chicago Press, 1998.

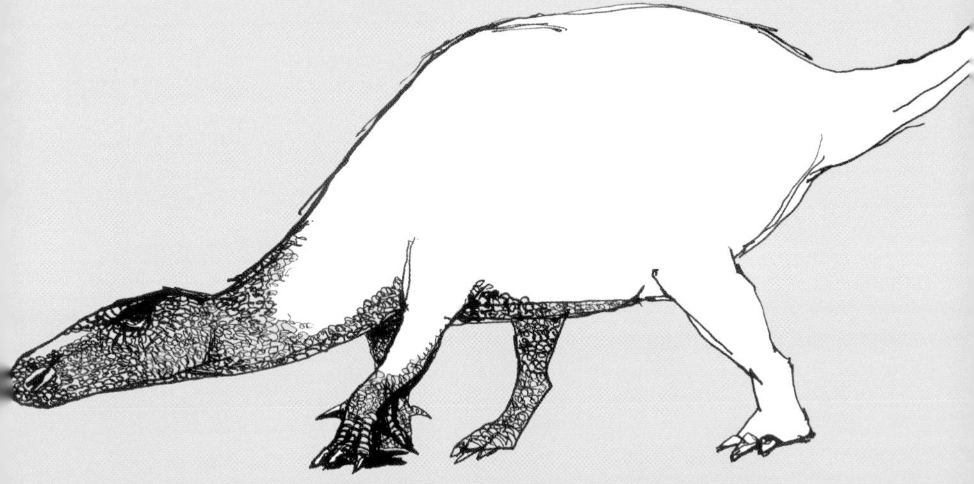

Where can you see dinosaurs?

Many museums have dinosaur skeletons on public display. The following list is only a selection, but with an emphasis on those museums showing genuine specimens rather than casts.

UNITED KINGDOM

BELFAST
Ulster Museum
Botanic Gardens
Belfast BT9 5AB
Tel: 028 90 383000
Reconstructed dinosaur and fossil trackway.

CAMBRIDGE
Sedgwick Museum
Department of Earth Sciences
University of Cambridge
Downing Street
Cambridge CB2 3EQ
Tel: 01223 333456
English dinosaurs.

DORCHESTER
Dinosaur Museum
Icen Way
Dorchester
Dorset
Tel: 01305 269880
The only museum in Britain dedicated solely to dinosaurs.

GLASGOW
Hunterian Museum and Art Gallery
University of Glasgow
Glasgow G12 8QQ
Tel: 0141 330 4221
Large collection of Jurassic marine reptile fossils, a reconstruction of a plesiosaur, and Gideon Mantell's own collection of dinosaur fossils.

LONDON
Natural History Museum
Cromwell Road
London SW7 5BD
Tel: 020 7942 5000
One of the largest collections of dinosaurs in Europe, with specimens from all over the world, including a recently-installed life-size model that moves and smells.

OXFORD
Oxford University Museum of Natural History
Parks Road
Oxford OX1 3PW
Tel: 01865 272950
Numerous remains of English dinosaurs, including the Megalosaurus, the first dinosaur to be described scientifically.

WHITBY
Whitby Museum
Pannet Park
Whitby
North Yorkshire
YO21 1RE
Tel: 01947 602908
Some specimens but mostly fossils from the Middle and Lower Jurassic periods, particularly marine reptiles, and slabs of rock with dinosaur footprints.

FRANCE

BOULOGNE-SUR-MER (PAS-DE-CALAIS)
Natural History Museum
Remains of dinosaurs from the Boulogne area.

ESPÉRAZA (AUDE)
Dinosaur Museum
The first French museum dedicated to dinosaurs, with a vast collection of dinosaurs from the South of France and from all over the world. Also offers the chance to visit sites of palaeontological excavations.

BELGIUM

BRUSSELS
Royal Museum of Natural Sciences of Belgium
In particular, it has an extraordinary collection of Iguanodon skeletons found in a mine at Bernissart in 1878.

GERMANY

BERLIN
Museum für Naturkunde
Especially dinosaurs from Tendaguru in Tanzania, including a Brachiosaurus, the largest dinosaur skeleton on display in the world.

FRANKFURT-AM-MAIN
Senckenberg-Museum
Dinosaurs from many parts of the world, including an exceptional natural 'mummy' of a Hadrosaurus

MUNICH
Bayerische Staatssammlung für Paläontologie und historische Geologie
Various dinosaurs, including specimens found in Bavaria.

STUTTGART
Staatliches Museum für Naturkunde
Vast collection of dinosaurs from the German Triassic.

SWITZERLAND

BASEL
Naturhistorisches Museum
Interesting collection of dinosaurs discovered in Switzerland.

PORTUGAL

LISBON
Geological Museum
Numerous dinosaur bones discovered in Portugal.

POLAND

WARSAW
Museum of Evolution
Fine collection of dinosaurs from the Gobi desert.

RUSSIA

MOSCOW
Institute of Palaeontology Museum
Numerous dinosaur skeletons from Central Asia.

CHINA

BEIJING
Palaeozoological Museum of the Institute of Palaeontology of Vertebrates
Large collection of dinosaur skeletons from various regions in China.

BEIJING
Natural History Museum
Good collection of Chinese dinosaurs.

ZIGONG (SICHUAN)
Dinosaur Museum
Remarkable site museum with skeletons of Jurassic dinosaurs exactly as they were found.

THAILAND

SAHATSAKHAN (KALASIN PROVINCE)
Wat Sakawan Dinosaur Museum
Remarkable site museum with sauropod skeletons still embedded in rock.

ARGENTINA

BUENOS AIRES
'Bernardino Rivadivia' Natural Science Museum of Argentina
Large collection of dinosaur skeletons recently discovered in Argentina.

UNITED STATES OF AMERICA

CHICAGO (ILLINOIS)
Field Museum of Natural History
Numerous spectacular skeletons of North American dinosaurs.

NEW HAVEN (CONNECTICUT)
Peabody Museum
A historic collection of dinosaurs from the western United States, begun in the 19th century.

NEW YORK
American Museum of Natural History
One of the largest collections of dinosaurs in the world, in a very modern display featuring dinosaurs from North America and Central Asia.

PITTSBURGH (PENNSYLVANIA)
Carnegie Museum
One of the great collections of North American dinosaurs.

VERNAL (UTAH)
Dinosaur National Monument
An amazing site museum where visitors can watch the updating of the skeletons of Jurassic dinosaurs.

WASHINGTON (D.C.)
National Museum of Natural History
Vast collection of North American dinosaur skeletons.

CANADA

DRUMHELLER (ALBERTA)
Royal Tyrrell Museum of Palaeontology
One of the largest permanent exhibitions of dinosaurs in the world.

OTTAWA (ONTARIO)
Canadian Museum of Nature
Fine collection of dinosaurs from the Cretaceous period found in western Canada.

TORONTO (ONTARIO)
Royal Ontario Museum
Very large collection of North American dinosaurs.

TUNISIA

TATOUINE
Musée de la mémoire de la Terre
Small museum showing remains of dinosaurs from rich deposits in southern Tunisia.

A

AMMONITES
Molluscs related to squids that were abundant throughout the Mesozoic period. The head and tentacles protruded from the open end of the shell, and they fed on smaller sea creatures.

ASTEROIDS
Small planets with wide-ranging diameters. The majority of asteroids in the solar system form a belt found between the orbits of Mars and Jupiter, but some have an orbit that enters the Earth's.

B

BELEMNITES
Molluscs related to squids that were common in the Mesozoic era. There bullet-shaped internal shells are usually found as fossils.

BENTHIC
Name given to living organisms on sea bed (or lake beds), as opposed to planktonic organisms that float in the water.

C

CALCAREOUS
Describes a rock that contains as much calcium carbonate as, for example, limestone or chalk.

CARBONIFEROUS
Penultimate period of the Palaeozoic era (360–295 million years ago), given this name because the rocks of this period contain large amounts of coal.

CATASTROPHISM
The theory that the history of the Earth has been punctuated by violent events causing a revolution in the animal and plant populations. Originally often based on religious beliefs, catastrophism was all but forgotten by main-stream science which tended to use gradual processes to account for many observations. Now, with the ascendancy of the idea of meteor impact as a cause of major extinctions, catastrophism is once more fashionable.

CENOZOIC
Geological era which began 65 million years ago and coincides with the development of mammals (from the Greek, meaning 'recent life').

COMET
An object in our solar system made up mainly of ice and rock, travelling in an elliptical orbit around the sun. When a comet approaches the sun it is partially vaporised, hence its 'tail'.

COMPARATIVE ANATOMY
The branch of biology that compares skeletons and other body parts of different organisms. Such studies may give clues to relationships and evolution. Comparative anatomy allows us to make predictions of dinosaur diets and lifestyles, based on comparisons with living animals.

CONTINENTAL DRIFT
The slow movement (of the order of one centimetre/0.5 inch per year) of huge blocks of the Earth's crust, driven by the molten rock below. Over millions of years the blocks, known to us as continents, have 'drifted' across the face of the Earth, at some periods being packed together (as in the early Mesozoic), and at others being well separated (as now).

CRETACEOUS
Third and last period of the Mesozoic era (135 – 65 million years ago), deriving its name from the Latin Creta, chalk, because it was during this period that the thick layers of chalk were formed in northern Europe.

D

DANIAN
The first geological age of the Palaeocene period, covering the first five million years or so after the end of the age of reptiles. It is named after Denmark, where rocks of this age are found.

F

FORAMINIFERA
Single cell marine organisms with calcareous shells. The accumulation of these often minuscule shells can produce rocky layers that are sometimes extremely thick.

G

GLACIATION
General cooling of the Earth's climate, during which the size of the polar ice caps and mountain glaciers increase considerably.

I

IRIDIUM
A metal of the platinum family which is very rarely found in terrestrial rocks, but more plentiful in certain meteorites. An unusually large quantity of iridium in a geological layer can therefore be a sign of a meteorite impact..

J

JURASSIC
Second period of the Mesozoic era, named after the Jura mountains in southern Germany, where rocks of this period have been found.

M

MESOZOIC

Geological era that began 250 million years ago and ended 65 million years ago (taken from two Greek words meaning 'middle life') characterised by the dominance of reptiles, and in particular of dinosaurs.

METEOR

A 'shooting star', extraterrestrial debris that hits the Earth's atmosphere and becomes incandescent with the effect of friction. Many meteors burn up completely. Sometimes the remains of larger bodies survive the journey through the atmosphere and hit the Earth's surface as a meteorite.

METEORITE

An object from interplanetary space that has reached the Earth. Depending on its origin, a meteorite may be largely stony, or alternatively, metallic with a high iron content.

N

NATURAL SELECTION

Often termed 'survival of the fittest'. The process by which animals and plants best adapted to their surroundings, survive and breed, while the poorly adapted fail. This selection acts as a filtering mechanism for the natural variations in organisms, and over generations, can lead to evolution of new types.

NICKELIFEROUS SPINELS

Magnetic minerals containing nickel, which are formed when a meteorite oxidises on entering the Earth's atmosphere. Their presence in a geological layer is a sign of a meteorite impact.

O

ORNITHISCIA

Group of dinosaurs with a four-branched pelvis similar to that of birds.

P

PALAEOZOIC

Geological era that began 540 million years ago and ended 250 million years ago (from two Greek words meaning 'ancient life'). The beginning of the Palaeozoic corresponded with a great expansion of animal life, which provided a large number of fossils.

PANGEA

Term applied to all the land above sea level at a time when all the continents were joined together in a single super-continent, as in the Permian and the Triassic periods.

PERMIAN

Last period of the Palaeozoic era (295–250 million years ago) named after the town of Perm in Russia, where rocks of this date are found.

S

SAURISCHIA

Group of dinosaurs characterised by a three-branched pelvis, similar to that of lizards.

SEDIMENTS

Deposits formed by the accumulation of mineral and rock fragments. The particles may also be of biological origin (shells, etc.).

SHOCKED QUARTZ

Mineral grain (quartz is silicon oxide) having undergone enormous pressure at the impact of a meteorite. Such shocked minerals are therefore a sign of impact.

T

TECTONIC PLATES

The plates which form the Earth's crust. Plate tectonics is the geological process by which these plates move against each other causing, amongst other things, continental drift.

TERTIARY PERIOD

The first part of the Cenozoic era. It began about sixty-five million years ago, when the Quaternary period started.

TRIASSIC

First period of the Mesozoic era (250-200 million years ago).

TYRANNOSAUR

A dinosaur of the family Tyrannosauridae, the most famous of which is Tyrannosaurus rex. Other tyrannosaurs include Albertosaurus and Gorgosaurus. they had large heads with serrated 'steak knife' teeth. They moved on their two huge hind legs, the tail balancing the body. The front legs were tiny by comparison.

U

UNIFORMITARIANISM

The belief that the geological changes of the past can be explained by the same gradual processes that are evident at the present day. Throughout time, rocks have weathered, eroded, been washed away and been deposited as sediments, whilst volcanoes have erupted and spread lava and ash. Geological change, and the accompanying evolution of animals and plants, have on the whole been gradual, ongoing processes.

Contents

Fact ⓫ 2–10

Discover » 11–50

Look » 51–64

In practice ⟫ 65–102

Find out ⟫ 103–125

Credits

Photographic Credits **P.13, 15, 19, 22, 24, 27, 31, 37, 51 to 64, 68–69** Eric Buffetaut – **P. 16**, © Photothèque Hachette – **P.21** ©John Reader/S.P.L./Cosmos – **P. 28–29**, D.R. – **P. 33**, © Vaughan Fleming/S. P. L./Cosmos– **P. 34**, © Chris Buler/S. P. L./Cosmos – **P. 39**, © DR David Kring/S. P. L./Cosmos – **P. 40**, © David Parker/S.P. L./Cosmos – **P. 42**, © Julian Baum/S. P. L./Cosmos – **P.45**, © Martin Land/ S. P. L./Cosmos – **P. 47**, © Louis Psihoyos/Matrix/Cosmos – **P. 48**, © Roger-Viollet – **P. 50**, © Mary Evans Picture Library – **P. 66–102**, Infographies: JSI – **P. 83**, © Jacana – **P. 96**, Chicxulub crater, ©S.P.L./Cosmos – **P. 102**, © Jacana – **P. 104–125**, Illustrations: Nicolas Hermlé– **P. 109**, © Phototèque Hachette – **P. 118–119**, © Christophe.

Acknowledgements

The author would like to thank the specialists in a variety of fields who, in conversation with him, have helped him to a better understanding of how dinosaurs came to be extinct. Particular thanks are due to: Robert Rocchia (CEA, Gif-sur-Yvette), Eric Robin (CEA, Gif-sur-Yvette), Jean Le Loeuff (Dinosaur Museum, Esperaza), Jan Smit (University of Amsterdam), Philippe Claeys (Natural History Museum, Berlin), Christian Koeberl (University of Vienna), Anne-Marie Lezine (National Scientific Research Centre, Paris).